THE GIGANTOMACHY OF SAMAISMELA

THE GIGANTOMACHY OF SAMAISMELA

Lawi S. Njeremani

Copyright © 2025 by PQADVANCEMENT PRESS

All rights reserved. No part of this publication may be reproduced, distributed, or transmitted in any form or by any means, including photocopying, recording, or other electronic or mechanical methods, without the prior written permission of the publisher, except in the case of brief quotations embodied in critical reviews and certain other noncommercial uses permitted by copyright law.

For permission requests, please contact the Publisher at Press@PQADVANCEMENT.ca

Every effort has been made to ensure the accuracy of the information presented in this book. However, errors or omissions may still exist. The author welcomes feedback from readers and encourages publishers to review any such discrepancies in order to rectify them in subsequent editions.

While the utmost care has been taken to provide reliable and up-to-date information, the author and publisher shall not be held liable for any unintentional errors or omissions or any damages arising from the use of this book. As a process of continuous engagement, we invite you to share any suggestions, feedback, new information, errors and omissions with the Publisher at Press@PQADVANCEMENT.ca

Thank you for respecting the author's work and for your understanding in contributing to the ongoing improvement of this literary endeavor. Your input is greatly valued.

Visit www.PQAdvancement.ca to read more about us, get links to our social media and subscribe to our alerts and updates as this book will be a continuous engagement, ensuring you are first to know of any new developments.

ISBN 978-1-0688139-1-7 (Paperback)
ISBN 978-1-0688139-2-4 (E-Book)
First Printing, 2025
PQADVANCEMENT PRESS
Ontario, Canada
www. PQADVANCEMENT.ca

DEDICATION

Consciousness, like a vaccine, must be administered to a significant quota of the populace to ensure herd-immunity against the ignoble subconscious and ignorant unconscious

CONTENTS

DEDICATION	iv
PREFACE	vi
SYNOPSIS	1
KEY ELEMENTS	4
STRUCTURE	6
CHARACTER DEVELOPMENT	13
1 ACT 1	23
2 ACT 2	32
3 ACT 3	39
4 ACT 4	45
5 ACT 5	58
6 ACT 6	68
ABOUT THE AUTHOR	71

PREFACE

The Gigantomachy of Samaismela is a dynamic stage play that reimagines the Greek myth of the Gigantomachy as a powerful allegory for the global and Kenyan struggle against systemic corruption. Set in the fictional nation of Samaismela—a vibrant stand-in for Kenya and other post-colonial societies—the play pits the Olympian gods, led by Zeus, and the mortal hero Heracles (symbolizing the Sovereigns, or global citizens) against Gaia's 12 Giants, each embodying a facet of corruption: bribery, tender cartels, electoral fraud, land grabs, judicial sabotage, cronyism, tax evasion, human trafficking, money laundering, county mismanagement, and drug trafficking. Through six acts of dialogue-driven drama, poetic performances, and mythic battles, the play explores the resilience of civic agency, the persistence of colonial legacies, and the urgent need for collective action to safeguard justice.

This text is designed for college-level courses in **Theater Studies**, **Literature, Political Science, African Studies, Post-Colonial Studies**, and **Ethics and Governance**. Its rich thematic tapestry, historical depth, and interactive elements—driven by a charismatic Narrator who engages the audience as Sovereigns—make it an ideal teaching tool for fostering critical analysis and performance-based learning. The play's integration of Kenyan milestones and global parallels (e.g., *Panama Papers*, *Trail of Tears*) offers students a lens to examine corruption's universal and localized impacts. Two original poems, "*The Nakedness of Truth*" and "*Oh Land o' Lilies*," serve as rallying cries for civic awakening, while the mysterious whistleblower, implied as the collective voice of the Sovereigns, underscores the power of grassroots activism.

***

SYNOPSIS

The Gigantomachy of Samaismela is a vibrant stage play that reimagines the ancient Greek myth of the Gigantomachy as a modern allegory for the struggle against corruption cartels, set in the fictional nation of Samaismela. Blending mythic grandeur with gritty realism, the play explores the battle between the Olympian gods, representing institutional justice, and the Giants, embodiments of corruption's many faces, with the citizens of Samaismela as the pivotal mortal force, akin to Heracles. Through dialogue-driven "battlefields" in courts and public squares, the play weaves philosophy, constitutional arguments drawn from Kenya's historical anti-corruption efforts, delivering a powerful narrative of collective awakening and systemic reform.

The curtains rise to the thunderous pulse of drums and cymbals, signaling the Titanomachy's final clash. Zeus, leading the 12 Olympians—Hera, Poseidon, Athena, Apollo, Artemis, Hephaestus, Hermes, Dionysus, Ares, Demeter, and Aphrodite—triumphs over the Titans.

One by one, the defeated Titans—Oceanus, Coeus, Crius, Hyperion, Iapetus, Cronus, Thea, Rhea, Themis, Mnemosyne, Phoebe, and Tethys—are cast into Tartarus' gaping maw, a dark abyss of solitude.

Gaia, draped in earthy hues, stands forlorn on blasted mounds, her head bowed. As the last Titan vanishes, she unleashes a piercing wail, vowing vengeance, and exits stage left to drum rolls.

In Tartarus, Gaia pleads with the abyssal deity to free the Titans for her revenge. Tartarus, a shadowy figure, resists, warning of repeated defeat. Desperate, Gaia insists on summoning new forces, but Tartarus rebuffs her. As she turns to leave, she pauses, a sly glint in her eye, and murmurs, "What if..." The curtains fall, leaving the audience in suspense.

The scene shifts to Heracles, staggering drunkenly onto the stage, embodying Samaismela's weary citizens. In celestial Olympia, Zeus, enthroned with lightning in hand, muses in soliloquy about his son's potential to endure life's trials—mirroring the citizens' capacity for heroism. Heracles tackles three of his Twelve Labors in rapid, symbolic succession, exiting stage left, a spark of resilience kindled.

Gaia reappears, weaving an enchantment over the Titanomachy's ruined mounds. They writhe and rise, forming the 12 Giants: Alcyoneus, Porphyrion, Enceladus, Mimas, Polybotes, Ephialtes, Pallas, Hippolytus, Gration, Thoon & Agrius (mythical twins) Eurytus, and Clytius.

Naming them, she sends them to Samaismela, a nation groaning under corruption cartels, colonial scars, injustice, and inequality. The Giants embody these vices, each a fictional character inspired by real-life corrupt cartel figures.

In Samaismela, the play unfolds across "battlefields" where dialogue, sharp with philosophical wit and rooted in contemporary and historic events, replaces swords. The Olympians, as institutional champions (e.g., Athena as the Judiciary, Hermes as the Anti-corruption Czar), clash with the Giants, who personify tender cartels (Porphyrion), bribe-takers (Alcyoneus), drug lords (Eurytus), opaque systems (Enceladus), and state & county mismanagement (Clytius). The citizens, dubbed the Sovereigns, rise as Heracles, their collective voice—through protests, poetry, and civic action—tipping the scales.

A narrator, a charismatic guide, stitches scenes with leading dialogue, contextualizing Samaismela's struggles with anti-corruption milestones. A mysterious whistleblower, unseen but pivotal, disrupts corrupt schemes, their revelations punctuating dialogues with damning leaks. The narrator challenges the audience: "Who is the whistleblower?

Can you unmask them?" This interactive element keeps viewers engaged, scanning for clues.

The play's climax sees the Sovereigns, Olympians, and whistleblower unite, not to eradicate corruption but to contain it, trapping the Giants like Enceladus under Etna. The moral lesson being eternal vigilance lest they erupt undetected. Through legal victories, public uprisings, and transparency reforms, Samaismela glimpses a new order, though the Giants' rumblings persist, demanding vigilance. The play closes with a call to the audience: to exercise direct sovereignty and active citizenship, wielding civic power to cage corruption's Titans and Giants.

***

KEY ELEMENTS

CHARACTERS:

Olympians (12): Zeus (justice's pinnacle), Hera (moral authority), Poseidon (legislative might), Athena (Judiciary), Apollo (truth's light), Artemis (civic purity), Hephaestus (institutional craft), Hermes (Anti-corruption Czar's cunning sting operations), Dionysus (youthful zeal), Ares (militant reform), Demeter (sustenance of equity), Aphrodite (social unity). Each embodies an anti-corruption force, with dialogue reflecting their mythic roles and Kenyan institutional realities.

Giants (12): Alcyoneus (bribe-takers), Porphyrion (tender cartels), Enceladus (systemic opacity), Mimas (electoral fraud), Polybotes (land grabbers), Ephialtes (judicial sabotage), Pallas (cronyism), Hippolytus (tax evasion), Gration (human trafficking), Thoon & Agrius (money laundering), Clytius (state & county mismanagement), Eurytus (drug lords). Fictional but inspired by real figures, they scheme in witty, villainous dialogues.

Gaia: The elite patronage nurturing corruption, a scheming matriarch.

Heracles: The Sovereigns, Samaismela's citizens, evolving from apathy to heroism.

Narrator: A charismatic commentator, blending humor and gravitas, linking scenes with historical parallels.

Whistleblower: A shadowy figure, their identity a mystery, disrupting Giant plots with leaks.

SETTING:

Samaismela, a vibrant, troubled nation with urban courts, raucous parliaments, and lively public squares, evoking its socio-political landscape. Olympia looms above, a celestial counterpoint.

***

STRUCTURE

ACT 1: THE SEEDS OF REVENGE

Setting: Cosmic battleground, Tartarus, and Olympia.

Synopsis: Establishes the mythic stakes and Samaismela's corruption. The Titanomachy ends with Zeus imprisoning the Titans, enraging Gaia, who vows revenge. In Tartarus, she births the 12 Giants to plague Samaismela. Heracles, symbolizing the Sovereigns, endures labors, reflecting civic struggles. The Narrator introduces the whistleblower mystery.

Key Events:
Scene 1: Zeus and Olympians cast Titans (Cronus, Rhea, etc.) into Tartarus; Gaia swears vengeance.
Scene 2: Gaia, rebuffed by Tartarus, creates the Giants alone.
Scene 3: Heracles' labors symbolize Sovereigns' resilience against poverty, corruption, and fear.
Scene 4: Gaia births the Giants (Alcyoneus, Porphyrion, etc.), who infiltrate Samaismela, embodying colonial and modern vices.

Characters: Zeus, Gaia, Heracles, Olympians, Titans, Tartarus, Giants, Narrator.

Historical Context: Titanomachy mirrors post-colonial betrayals; Giants reflect scandals and global corruption.

Significance: Sets up the conflict, introduces Samaismela as a corrupted nation, and positions Heracles as the prophecy's mortal hero.

***

ACT 2: THE STIRRINGS OF WAR

Setting: Olympia's gardens and Samaismela's lush meadow.

Synopsis: The Olympians detect tremors in Samaismela, suspecting Gaia's Giants. Poseidon accuses Athena, Artemis blames Apollo, and Hermes hints at seeing Gaia near Tartarus, sparking rivalry and urgency. The Giants, posing for a portrait, boast of dominating Samaismela's institutions. The whistleblower's off-stage whistle heightens tension.

Key Events:
Scene 1: In Olympia, Poseidon reports sea tremors, Hermes reveals Gaia's Tartarus visit, and Zeus declares war as the "*Rhythm Tate-taa-taa*" chant emerges.
Scene 2: In Samaismela, the Giants (Alcyoneus, Porphyrion, etc.) recount their corrupt triumphs (e.g., rigged elections, land grabs), posing for a portrait disrupted by a whistle, the "*Rhythm Tate-taa-taa*" chant.

Characters: Zeus, Poseidon, Athena, Hermes, Apollo, Artemis, Dionysus, other Olympians, Giants, Narrator.

Historical Context: Olympian rivalries echo institutional clashes (Executive vs. Parliament, etc); Giants' boasts cite election fraud, colonial land grabs, and Panama Papers.

Significance: Escalates the conflict, showing the Giants' grip on Samaismela and the Olympians' resolve, with the whistleblower as a growing force.

ACT 3: THE COSMIC CONFRONTATION

Setting: Samaismela's lush meadow with Tartarus' pit.

Synopsis: Zeus confronts Gaia, who defends her Titans and Giants, rejecting his justice. Heracles asserts free will, denying Zeus' fatherhood, while Hades warns against Tartarus' acid. Alcyoneus taunts Zeus, boasting of the Giants' enduring influence (e.g., Mau Mau's defeat, apartheid's subtler chains), declaring war. The Narrator teases the prophecy's mortal hero.

Key Events:
Scene 1: Gaia waltzes, clashing with Zeus over Cronus and free will; Heracles debates Zeus on equality; Hades rebuffs soul-sharing; Alcyoneus challenges Zeus, citing global corruption, triggering war trumpets.

Characters: Zeus, Gaia, Heracles, Hades, Alcyoneus, other Giants, Narrator.

Historical Context: Gaia's defiance mirrors elite resistance from political dynasties; Alcyoneus' speech references Martin Luther, Dedan Kimathi, and global systemic vices (tax havens, trafficking).

Significance: Deepens philosophical stakes (free will vs. corruption), primes battlefields, and positions Heracles as Samaismela's champion.

***

ACT 4: THE BATTLEFIELDS IGNITE

Setting: Samaismela's courtroom, warehouse, high ground, dock, and lush landscape.

Synopsis: The Olympians and Heracles engage the Giants across Samaismela's institutions, felling seven in symbolic battles. Zeus loses a courtroom case against Alcyoneus' land grabs, but Athena traps Enceladus with evidence. Hephaestus crushes Mimas' vote fraud, Poseidon drowns Polybotes' land claims, and Hermes chases Hippolytus' tax evasion. Heracles, reciting *"The Nakedness of Truth,"* leads Zeus, Apollo, and Hecate (Demeter's ally) to defeat Porphyrion, Ephialtes, and Clytius. The whistleblower's leaks escalate, and the Narrator urges audience heroism.

Key Events:
Scene 1: Zeus accuses Giants of colonial land injustices (Maasai, Cherokee); Alcyoneus defends "civilizing" colonization; Ephialtes bribes the judge, dismissing the case. Athena confronts Enceladus over narcotics and judicial dinners, vowing evidence.
Scene 2: Hephaestus catches Mimas rigging votes, ending his fraud.
Scene 3: Poseidon challenges Polybotes' land grabs, reclaiming communal rights.
Scene 4: Hermes, disguised as Hades, traps Hippolytus sealing tax-haven wealth.
Scene 5: Heracles recites *"The Nakedness of Truth,"* orchestrating Porphyrion's (cartels), Ephialtes' (judicial sabotage), and Clytius' (mismanagement) falls into Tartarus.

Characters: Zeus, Athena, Hephaestus, Poseidon, Hermes, Heracles, Hecate, Giants, Judge, Sovereigns, Narrator.

Historical Context: Courtroom evokes judicial scandals and colonial evictions; Enceladus' fall cites Rothstein's rackets and Kenya's opaque budgets; Mimas mirrors 2007 election fraud; Polybotes recalls Highlands grabs; Hippolytus reflects Panama Papers; Scene 5 nods to judicial reforms, and state & county audits.

Significance: Shows corruption's varied arenas (courts, elections, lands, finance), with Heracles' poetry and Sovereigns' activism (smartphones, placards) driving victories, though Alcyoneus remains.

***

ACT 5: THE SOVEREIGNS' TRIUMPH

Setting: Olympia's plenary court and Samaismela's public square.

Synopsis: Heracles, declared the prophecy's mortal, strategizes in Olympia, requesting Artemis, Dionysus, Athena, and the Moirai to end the Gigantomachy. In Samaismela's vibrant square, he recites "*Oh Land o' Lilies*," rallying Sovereigns as the Moirai, Dionysus, Athena, and Artemis orchestrate the falls of the twins Thoon & Agrius, Eurytus, Pallas, and Gration into Tartarus. Alcyoneus, defiant, boasts of corruption's enduring grip (greed, apathy), but Heracles fells him, proclaiming Samaismela's sovereignty. The Narrator positions the audience as the prophecy's mortals, urging civic duty.

Key Events:

Scene 1: In Olympia, Heracles, having completed his labors, requests Artemis, Dionysus, Athena, and the Moirai, keeping his plan secret to avoid rivalries.

Scene 2: In Samaismela, Heracles chants "Oh Land o' Lilies," defeating Thoon & Agrius (money laundering), Eurytus (drugs), Pallas (cronyism), and Gration (trafficking). Alcyoneus warns of ongoing vices, but Heracles, noting Samaismela's ground, sends him to Tartarus amid Sovereigns' ululation.

Characters: Heracles, Zeus, Hera, Athena, Hermes, Ares, Artemis, Dionysus, Moirai, Giants, Sovereigns, Narrator.

Historical Context: Heracles' strategy reflects civic movements (budget forums, Constitutionalism); Giant defeats evoke drug busts, parastatal reforms, anti-trafficking efforts, and constitutional accountability. Alcyoneus' speech cites global apathy (low voter turnout, selective justice) and government financial scandals.

Significance: Climaxes with Heracles and Sovereigns as civic heroes, defeating all Giants but warning of corruption's resilience, with "*Rhythm Tate-taa-taa!*" whistle chants tying to activism.

***

ACT 6: THE CALL TO PROTECT

Setting: Olympia's gardens.

Synopsis: In a triumphant yet urgent epilogue, the Olympians, including Hades and Poseidon, celebrate the Gigantomachy's end. Zeus, with Heracles (now in golden-white lion headgear), reveals a threat:

someone hunts the whistleblower, implied as the Sovereigns' collective voice. Rallying the Olympians to march to Samaismela, Zeus leads them to protect this vital force, set to the rhythmic *"Rhythm Tate-taa-taa"* chant. The play ends in darkness, urging audience vigilance.

Key Events:
Scene 1: Olympians rejoice; Zeus announces the whistleblower's endangerment, leading a unified march to Samaismela with Heracles, accompanied by whistles and *"Rhythm Tate-taa-taa"* chants.

Characters: Zeus, Heracles, Hera, Poseidon, Athena, Apollo, Artemis, Hephaestus, Hermes, Dionysus, Ares, Demeter, Aphrodite, Hades, Narrator.

Historical Context: Whistleblower's threat mirrors real-world retaliation; *"Rhythm Tate-taa-taa"* evokes protest culture; ten-year cycle nods to recurring crises (electoral, racist and segregationist violence, global scandals).

Significance: Concludes with a call to protect civic courage, positioning the audience as Sovereigns tasked with sustaining Samaismela's victory, leaving the whistleblower's identity collective and universal.

***

CHARACTER DEVELOPMENT

Below is a detailed character development guide for the 12 Giants, Gaia, Heracles, and the 12 Olympians in *The Gigantomachy of Samaismela*, a stage play that reimagines the Greek myth as a global allegory for the fight against corruption cartels.

The Giants are personifications of systemic vices, drawing from historical figures and events across the world, while the Olympians represent institutional and moral forces of justice. Heracles embodies the collective power of global citizens (the Sovereigns), and Gaia symbolizes entrenched elite patronage. Each character is crafted to deliver witty, argumentative dialogue in dialogue-driven "battlefields", blending mythic grandeur with historical realism.

***

GIANTS (OFFSPRING OF GAIA)

The 12 Giants are colossal, serpentine-legged figures, each embodying a form of corruption or societal vice. Their personalities and dialogues reflect the cunning, arrogance, and resilience of their historical inspirations, drawn from global and Kenyan contexts. They scheme with Machiavellian flair, their arguments laced with historical references and self-justifying rhetoric, but face opposition from the Olympians and Sovereigns.

***

1. ALCYONEUS (BRIBE-TAKERS)

Mythic Role: Leader of the Giants, immortal in his homeland until dragged away by Heracles.

Representation: Historical colonizers who extracted wealth through coercion and bribery, such as Lord Delamere (3rd Baron, Kenyan settler elite), Lord Kitchener (impaler of the Mahdi revolt and Boer War), Cecil Rhodes (British imperialist), John Cabot (explorer-exploiter), Captain James Cook (Pacific colonizer), William Bradford (Plymouth governor), and Major General Philip Sheridan (Native American displacement).

Personality: Charismatic, imperious, with a silver tongue that masks ruthless greed. He justifies bribery as "necessary for progress," citing colonial "civilizing missions."

Dialogue Style: Smooth, persuasive, with veiled threats. E.g., "Gold greases empires, Sovereigns—ranches, mines, all built on sweet deals."

Stage Presence: Draped in colonial regalia (e.g., pith helmet, medals), wielding a ledger of bribes.

Conflict: Faces Zeus in court, defending bribe networks, and Sovereigns, who expose his global analogues.

2. PORPHYRION (TENDER CARTELS)

Mythic Role: Chief Giant, targeting Zeus and Hera, felled by Zeus and Heracles.

Representation: Industrial magnates who rigged systems, like Ewart Grogan (Kenyan settler-tycoon), John D. Rockefeller (Standard Oil), and J.P. Morgan (banking monopolist).

Personality: Arrogant, strategic, viewing governments as pawns. He boasts of "building nations" while rigging tenders.

Dialogue Style: Booming, laced with capitalist bravado. E.g., "Rockefeller's oil, Vanderbilt's railways—my cartels fuel progress, Zeus!"

Stage Presence: In a tailored suit with gold chains, clutching contracts.

Conflict: Clashes with Zeus (justice) and Sovereigns while defending tender scams.

3. ENCELADUS (SYSTEMIC OPACITY)

Mythic Role: Buried under Mount Etna by Athena.

Representation: Figures thriving in opaque systems, like Boss Tweed and Timothy Sullivan (Tammany Hall), Mayer Rothschild (banking secrecy), and Jimmy Hoffa (Teamsters' corruption).

Personality: Secretive, manipulative, cloaking deeds in bureaucratic fog.

Dialogue Style: Evasive, with doublespeak. E.g., "Transparency? Tweed's New York thrived in shadows, Athena."

Stage Presence: In a dark cloak, surrounded by fog, holding sealed ledgers.

Conflict: Faces Athena and Sovereigns in public squares, resisting transparency demands

4. MIMAS (ELECTORAL FRAUD)

Mythic Role: Crushed by Hephaestus' molten metal.

Representation: Electoral fraudsters globally, from Mexico's 1988 elections, Kenya's, Malaysia's and Pakistan's elections, Cambodia's 2018 elections, Bolivia's 2019 elections, Kyrgyzstan's 2020 elections, Georgia's and Venezuela's 2024 elections, to historical carousel voting and vote-buyers like 19th-century American political machines and the Soviet axis voting systems.

Personality: Deceptive, theatrical, rigging votes with a showman's grin.

Dialogue Style: Fast-talking, populist. E.g., "Votes are clay, Hephaestus—I mold them to serve!"

Stage Presence: In a garish campaign outfit, tossing fake ballots.

Conflict: Battles Hephaestus (institutional reform) and Sovereigns in electoral tribunals, defending fraud.

5. POLYBOTES (LAND GRABBERS)

Mythic Role: Crushed under Kos by Poseidon.

Representation: Colonists associations (e.g., British Empire's settler groups), post-colonial governments, and European settlers in Africa, Australia, North & South America

Personality: Territorial, entitled, claiming land as a birthright.

Dialogue Style: Imperial, possessive. E.g., "These lands were empty before us, Poseidon—ask the settlers!"

Stage Presence: In settler garb, clutching land deeds.

Conflict: Faces Poseidon (legislation) and Sovereigns in land reform hearings, resisting restitution.

6. EPHIALTES (JUDICIAL SABOTAGE)

Mythic Role: Struck by Apollo and Heracles' arrows.

Representation: Corrupt judges globally, enriching themselves through bribes and rulings.

Personality: Hypocritical, cloaking corruption in legal jargon.

Dialogue Style: Erudite, self-righteous. E.g., "Justice bends to gold, Apollo—every gavel has its price."

Stage Presence: In judicial robes, stained with gold dust.

Conflict: Clashes with Apollo (truth) and Sovereigns in court, defending rigged judgments.

7. PALLAS (CRONYISM)

Mythic Role: Flayed by Athena, skin used as a shield.

Representation: Public officials granting favors to allies, from state and public service appointments to global patronage networks.

Personality: Charming, nepotistic, rewarding loyalty over merit.

Dialogue Style: Warm, manipulative. E.g., "Friends lift empires, Athena—why else do boards exist?"

Stage Presence: In a flashy suit, handing out favors.

Conflict: Faces Athena and Sovereigns in oversight hearings, justifying crony hires.

8. HIPPOLYTUS (TAX EVASION)

Mythic Role: Killed by Hermes with Hades' helm.

Representation: Prominent tax evaders, from historical figures to modern offshore schemers (e.g., Panama & Pandora Papers figures).

Personality: Elusive, smug, hiding wealth in shadows.

Dialogue Style: Clever, dismissive. E.g., "Taxes are for fools, Hermes—my gold sails to Caymans."

Stage Presence: In a sleek suit, clutching offshore bank files.

Conflict: Battles Hermes (Anti-Corruption Czar) and Sovereigns in tax audits, dodging accountability (e.g. tax haven leaks).

9. GRATION (HUMAN TRAFFICKING)

Mythic Role: Slain by Artemis' arrows.

Representation: Human traffickers in Central/South America, Europe, Asia, and North Africa (e.g., global smuggling rings).

Personality: Cruel, predatory, exploiting desperation.

Dialogue Style: Cold, transactional. E.g., "Borders are profit, Artemis—humans are cargo."

Stage Presence: In a hooded cloak, with chains.

Conflict: Faces Artemis (civic purity) and Sovereigns in public campaigns, exposing trafficking (e.g., global anti-slavery movements).

10. THOON & AGRIUS (MONEY LAUNDERING)

Mythic Role: Killed by the Moirai (adapted as Hermes' ally).

Representation: Money-laundering banks, tax havens, and mob figures like Al Capone, Meyer Lansky, Arnold Rothstein, Lucky Luciano, Frank Costello.

Personality: Calculating, urbane, washing blood money clean.

Dialogue Style: Slick, technical. E.g., "Dirty coin sparkles in my banks, Hermes—Rothstein was my favorite."

Stage Presence: In a pinstripe suit and fedora, with stacks of cash.

Conflict: Clashes with Hermes and Sovereigns in financial probes, defending laundered funds (e.g., banking scandals).

11. CLYTIUS (STATE & COUNTY MISMANAGEMENT)

Mythic Role: Destroyed by Hecate and Heracles (adapted as Demeter's ally).

Representation: Mismanaged state, regional, and local governments, from local counties to global examples.

Personality: Incompetent, wasteful, blaming others.

Dialogue Style: Defensive, bureaucratic. E.g., "Budgets vanish, Demeter— states, provinces and counties aren't meant to thrive!"

Stage Presence: In a disheveled official's uniform, with mismanaged files.

Conflict: Faces Demeter (equity) and Sovereigns in budget forums, defending waste (e.g., Kenya's state & county audits).

12. EURYTUS (DRUG LORDS)

Mythic Role: Slain by Dionysus.

Representation: Drug lords like El Chapo, Tse Chi Lop, Pablo Escobar, Ibrahim Akasha, Vicky Goswami, Muhammed Asif Hafiz a.k.a "Sultan", The Kinahan Transnational Criminal Organization (KTCO).

Personality: Ruthless, charismatic, peddling poison as power.

Dialogue Style: Menacing, seductive. E.g., "My powder rules streets, Dionysus—Escobar's legacy lives!"

Stage Presence: In a narco-lord's attire, with drug caches.

Conflict: Battles Dionysus (youthful zeal) and Sovereigns in anti-drug campaigns, resisting busts.

***

GAIA (PRIMORDIAL INSTIGATOR)

Mythic Role: Mother of the Giants, inciting their revolt against the Olympians.

Representation: Global elite patronage, from political dynasties to international oligarchs, nurturing corruption's roots.

Personality: Scheming, maternal, fiercely protective of her "children" (Giants). She justifies corruption as a natural order born of a disrupted cosmos.

Dialogue Style: Poetic, manipulative. E.g., "My Giants are progress, Zeus—empires rise on their backs."

Stage Presence: Draped in earthy, regal robes, standing on shifting mounds, her voice resonant with ancient power.

Conflict: Orchestrates the Giants' schemes from behind the scenes, confronting Zeus in a climactic dialogue about power's cost.

***

HERACLES (THE SOVEREIGNS)
Mythic Role: Mortal hero, essential to the Olympians' victory, slaying Giants with his arrows.

Representation: Global citizens, particularly Samaismela's Sovereigns, embodying collective civic power. Inspired by local activists, global whistleblowers, and movements like the Gen Z protests, "Occupy movement", The Gwangju Uprising, Sri Lanka's Uprising, The George Floyd protests or Arab Spring.

Personality: Initially weary, disillusioned, evolving into resolute, unified heroism.

Dialogue Style: Raw, evolving from lament to eloquence. E.g., "We've bled enough, Alcyoneus—our voice will bury you!"

Stage Presence: A chorus of diverse figures (farmers, students, workers), wielding placards, smartphones, and constitutional texts.

Conflict: Battles each Giant alongside Olympians, using protests, poetry and leaks to expose corruption cartels.

***

OLYMPIAN GODS (12)
The Olympians are celestial champions of justice, each representing an anti-corruption force. Their dialogues blend mythic gravitas with modern institutional logic, drawing from global and Kenyan reform efforts. They evolve from aloof deities to partners of the Sovereigns, reflecting the need for institutional-citizen synergy.

1. ZEUS (JUSTICE'S PINNACLE)
Role: Leads the Olympians, wielding thunderbolts.

Representation: Supreme justice, inspired by global constitutional courts.

Personality: Authoritative, burdened by responsibility.

Dialogue: Commanding, principled. E.g., "Did you think the Maasai, Cherokee, or Navajo wouldn't return?"
Conflict: Faces Alcyoneus in legal battles, pushing anti-cartel petitions.

2. HERA (MORAL AUTHORITY)
Role: Defends divine order.
Representation: Ethical leadership, like constitutional integrity clauses.
Personality: Stern, compassionate.
Dialogue: Moral, cutting. E.g., "Enough games, Hermes!"
Conflict: Challenges Pallas in oversight hearings.

3. POSEIDON (LEGISLATIVE MIGHT)
Role: Crushes Polybotes with an island.
Representation: Parliaments passing reform laws.
Personality: Forceful, pragmatic.
Dialogue: Robust, policy-driven. E.g., "Polybotes, land reforms will drown your greed!"
Conflict: Battles Polybotes in land reform debates.

4. ATHENA (JUDICIARY)
Role: Buries Enceladus, flays Pallas.
Representation: Independent judiciary.
Personality: Wise, resolute.
Dialogue: Logical, constitutional. E.g., "Enceladus, transparency is my shield!"
Conflict: Faces Enceladus and Ephialtes in court.

5. APOLLO (TRUTH'S LIGHT)
Role: Shoots Ephialtes.
Representation: Investigative journalism and truth-seekers.
Personality: Piercing, idealistic.

Dialogue: Exposing, poetic. E.g., "Ephialtes, my light burns your lies!"

Conflict: Exposes Ephialtes' judicial corruption.

6. ARTEMIS (CIVIC PURITY)
Role: Slays Gration.
Representation: Youth and civic movements.
Personality: Fierce, untamed.
Dialogue: Passionate and confident. E.g., "I missed a stag—an easy shot—when the earth shuddered beneath me."
Conflict: Leads Sovereigns against Gration in anti-trafficking campaigns.

7. HEPHAESTUS (INSTITUTIONAL CRAFT)
Role: Crushes Mimas.
Representation: Electoral reforms and institutions.
Personality: Methodical, innovative.
Dialogue: Technical, determined. E.g., "Mimas, my systems will purify your fraud!"
Conflict: Battles Mimas in electoral tribunals.

8. HERMES (ANTI-CORRUPTION CZAR'S CUNNING)
Role: Kills Hippolytus with Hades' helm.
Representation: Anti-corruption agencies globally.
Personality: Sly, relentless.
Dialogue: Sharp, investigative. E.g., "Hippolytus, your tax havens can't hide from me!"
Conflict: Pursues Hippolytus, Thoon and his twin Agrius in audits.

9. DIONYSUS (YOUTHFUL ZEAL)
Role: Slays Eurytus.
Representation: Grassroots anti-drug movements.
Personality: Vibrant, rebellious, witty.

Dialogue: Fiery, charismatic. E.g., "I've heard whistles in Samaismela—sharp, piercing. I thought it was my vintage, potent from Titanomachy's chaos."
Conflict: Rallies Sovereigns against Eurytus.

10. ARES (MILITANT REFORM)
Role: Fights Giants broadly.
Representation: Aggressive anti-corruption campaigns.
Personality: Bold, confrontational.
Dialogue: Martial, direct.
Conflict: Supports Sovereigns against Clytius.

11. DEMETER (SUSTENANCE OF EQUITY)
Role: Fights with a sickle (adapted).
Representation: Economic justice and fair resource allocation.
Personality: Nurturing, steadfast.
Dialogue: Grounded, equitable. E.g., "Clytius, states, provinces and counties must serve, not steal!"
Conflict: Challenges Clytius in budget forums.

12. APHRODITE (SOCIAL UNITY)
Role: Unites gods (adapted).
Representation: Social cohesion against corruption's divisiveness.
Personality: Charismatic, unifying.
Dialogue: Persuasive, inclusive. E.g., "Sovereigns, unite against Alcyoneus' bribes!"
Conflict: Rallies Sovereigns against Alcyoneus' divisive tactics.

***

ACT 1

SCENE 1 - THE SEEDS OF REVENGE

Setting: A cosmic stage divided into three realms: the blasted battleground of the Titanomachy, the dark abyss of Tartarus, and celestial Olympia. Mounds of earth, scorched and jagged, dot the foreground. A gaping, smoky pit (Tartarus) looms center-stage. Above, Olympia glimmers with ethereal light, a raised throne for Zeus. The air hums with tension, underscored by rhythmic drums and cymbals.

Characters in Act 1:

- **Olympians**: Zeus, Hera, Poseidon, Athena, Apollo, Artemis, Hephaestus, Hermes, Dionysus, Ares, Demeter, Aphrodite.
- **Titans**: Oceanus, Coeus, Crius, Hyperion, Iapetus, Cronus, Thea, Rhea, Themis, Mnemosyne, Phoebe, Tethys (non-speaking, symbolic).
- **Gaia**: Earth Mother, elite patronage.
- **Tartarus**: Abyssal deity.
- **Heracles**: The Sovereigns, global citizens.
- **Narrator**: Charismatic guide, linking myth and history.
- **Giants** (introduced at end): Alcyoneus, Porphyrion, Enceladus, Mimas, Polybotes, Ephialtes, Pallas, Hippolytus, Gration, Thoon & Agrius, Clytius, Eurytus.

***

[*Lights up. The stage pulses with DRUMS and STACCATO CYMBALS, evoking a cosmic war. Smoke swirls across the battleground. The 12 OLYMPIANS stand triumphant, their celestial armor gleaming. ZEUS, lightning in hand, stands center, flanked by HERA, POSEIDON, ATHENA, and others. The defeated TITANS, shadowy figures in chains, kneel before the pit of Tartarus. GAIA, draped in earthy robes, stands stage left on a mound, head bowed, her presence heavy with sorrow. The NARRATOR enters stage right, vibrant and commanding.*]

NARRATOR: (*To audience, with a knowing grin*) Welcome, seekers of truth, to a tale as old as mountains, yet as fresh as today's headlines. Behold the Gigantomachy, where gods and mortals clash to tame chaos. But this is no mere myth—it's Samaismela's saga, a nation like our own, scarred by corruption cartels, yearning for justice. Watch closely, for history whispers here, from streets to empires past. Keep your eyes sharp! (*Gestures to the stage*) The Titanomachy ends, and a new war brews...

[*DRUMS intensify. ZEUS steps forward, his voice thunderous.*]

ZEUS: Olympians, we stand victorious! The Titans, our kin, dared defy the cosmos' order. Now, they face eternity's judgment. Name them, Athena, as we cast them to Tartarus!
ATHENA: (*Stepping forward, scroll in hand, resolute*) Oceanus, lord of rivers, who drowned justice in ambition.

[*OCEANUS, a towering figure, is dragged to the pit by ARES and APOLLO. He vanishes into the smoky maw with a wail. GAIA flinches, clutching her mound.*]

ATHENA: Coeus, star-gazer, who twisted wisdom to treason.

[COEUS follows, pushed by HERMES and DIONYSUS. GAIA's hands tremble.]

ATHENA: Crius, Hyperion, Iapetus—warriors of shadow, fallen to hubris.

[The three TITANS are cast in quick succession, each vanishing with a cry. The DRUMS pulse faster.]

ATHENA: Cronus, father-tyrant, who devoured his own to cling to power.

[CRONUS, massive and defiant, is shoved by POSEIDON and HEPHAESTUS. His roar echoes as he falls. GAIA staggers, her face contorted.]

ATHENA: Thea, Rhea, Themis, Mnemosyne, Phoebe, Tethys—sisters who wove chaos' thread.

[The six TITANESS figures, veiled and silent, are led to the pit by ARTEMIS, DEMETER, and APHRODITE. They vanish in a swirl of smoke. GAIA collapses to her knees, letting out a piercing WAIL that silences the DRUMS.]

GAIA: (*Rising, voice raw with fury*) Zeus, you cage my children, but the earth remembers! Your throne will crumble, your justice rot! I swear vengeance—a storm to shake Olympia itself!

[GAIA sweeps off stage left, her robes trailing like roots. The OLYMPIANS stand firm, but ZEUS' eyes narrow. DRUM ROLLS crescendo as the CURTAINS CLOSE.]

***

SCENE 2: TARTARUS' DEPTHS

[Lights dim to an eerie glow. The stage is a cavernous void, with jagged rocks and swirling mist. TARTARUS, a shadowy, towering figure cloaked in darkness, looms center. GAIA enters from stage left, her earthy robes stark against the abyss. The NARRATOR steps forward, stage right.]

NARRATOR: (*To audience*) Deep in Tartarus, where light dares not linger, Gaia schemes. Her heart burns for her Titans, but the abyss is no ally. Watch her weave a new plot—one that echoes from ancient grudges to modern Samaismela, where corruption festers like a wound. Who will rise to meet her?

[GAIA approaches TARTARUS, her voice pleading yet fierce.]

GAIA: Tartarus, father of shadows, hear me! Free my Titans—Oceanus, Cronus, Rhea—let them storm Olympia and crush Zeus' tyranny!

TARTARUS: (*Voice low, resonant*) Gaia, your Titans fell before. They challenged the gods and withered. Why repeat their doom?

GAIA: (*Stepping closer, eyes blazing*) Because I am the Earth, eternal! My might will birth a vengeance Zeus cannot fathom. Free them, and I'll reshape the cosmos!

TARTARUS: (**Unmoved**) Your love blinds you. The Olympians are no mere sparks—they are fire. Another war, and your children face worse than chains.

[GAIA paces, her hands clenching. She pauses, then turns, desperation sharpening her tone.]

GAIA: Then give me new children, Tartarus! Ones fiercer than Titans, born of earth and abyss, to tear down Zeus' order!

TARTARUS: (*Laughs darkly*) You ask too much, Gaia. Such a brood would rend the world, not rule it. Begone—your grief is not my burden.

[GAIA starts to exit stage left, shoulders slumped. She halts, a sly smile creeping across her face. She turns back, voice soft but cunning.]

GAIA: What if... I craft them myself? Not Titans, but Giants—born of my will alone, to plague not just Olympia, but the mortal world below?

[TARTARUS' eyes glint, intrigued. He nods slowly. GAIA's smile widens as the LIGHTS FADE. CURTAINS CLOSE to a haunting CYMBAL CRASH.]

***

SCENE 3: HERACLES' LABORS

[Lights rise on a vibrant, earthly stage, symbolizing Samaismela and the global mortal realm. A raised throne in celestial OLYMPIA glows above, where ZEUS sits, lightning in hand. HERACLES, representing the SOVEREIGNS, enters stage right in a drunken stupor, ragged but resilient, a chorus of diverse figures (farmers, students, workers) behind him. The NARRATOR strides in, stage left.]

NARRATOR: (*To audience*) From divine wars to mortal struggles, we turn to Heracles—Samaismela's Sovereigns, the people of every land, from slums to mega streets. Wounded by injustice, they stagger, yet their spirit endures. Zeus watches his son, pondering: can mortals rise without gods? (*Gestures to Heracles*) Behold his labors, trials that forge heroes.

[*ZEUS rises, gazing down at HERACLES. The DRUMS soften to a heartbeat rhythm.*]

ZEUS: (*Soliloquy, voice heavy*) Heracles, my son, born of mortal clay yet divine fire. Samaismela groans under the weight of corruption cartels—tenders, bribes, stolen lands. Your labors test you: can you rise without my thunder? The Sovereigns falter, divided by tribe and greed, yet in you, I see a spark. Endure, and you may yet shake the Giants I dread.

[*HERACLES stumbles center-stage, the SOVEREIGNS echoing his movements. Three LABORS unfold in quick, symbolic tableaux, accompanied by SPORADIC DRUMMING and CYMBALS.*]

SOVEREIGN 1: (*As Heracles slays the Nemean Lion*) We battle poverty's claws, clawing at our dreams!

[*HERACLES wrestles a lion-puppet, tearing its hide. The SOVEREIGNS cheer, growing bolder.*]

SOVEREIGN 2: (*As Heracles slays the Hydra*) We cut corruption's heads, though they regrow!

[*HERACLES slashes a multi-headed Hydra prop, each head regenerating until he burns them. The SOVEREIGNS wield torches, united.*]

SOVEREIGN 3: (*As Heracles captures the Cerberus*) We face fear's hounds—violence, betrayal—yet we chain them!

[*HERACLES drags a three-headed dog prop, chaining it. The SOVEREIGNS raise fists, exiting stage left with renewed purpose. ZEUS nods, a flicker of hope in his eyes. CURTAINS CLOSE to a triumphant DRUM ROLL MATCH.]*

***

SCENE 4: THE BIRTH OF THE GIANTS

[Lights rise on a desolate stage, the Titanomachy's mounds pulsing with eerie green light. GAIA stands center, her robes flowing like roots. The NARRATOR enters stage right, voice low and urgent.]

NARRATOR: (*To audience*) Gaia, spurned by Tartarus, turns to her own power. From earth's wounds, she births monsters—not Titans, but Giants, each a vice that plagues Samaismela and our world. Their names echo history's villains, from colonial plunderers to modern schemers. Watch as corruption takes form, and ask: who will stand against them?

[GAIA raises her arms, chanting an ENCHANTMENT. The mounds quake, rising into the 12 GIANTS, their serpentine legs coiling, costumes reflecting their vices: ALCYONEUS in colonial medals, PORPHYRION in a gold-chained suit, ENCELADUS cloaked in fog, and so on. DRUMS pulse ominously.]

GAIA: (*Voice resonant*) Earth, my flesh, birth my vengeance! From Titanomachy's scars, rise my Giants, each a scourge to Olympia and mortals below! Alcyoneus, bribe-taker, progenitor to Rhodes, Kitchener and Delamere!

[ALCYONEUS steps forward, grinning, clutching a ledger.]

ALCYONEUS: Gold bends knees, Mother—empires kneel to my coin!

GAIA: Porphyrion, cartel-lord, kin to Rockefeller, Vanderbilt and Grogan!

[PORPHYRION strides forth, contracts in hand.]

PORPHYRION: Tenders are mine, Gaia—governments dance to my tune!

GAIA: Enceladus, shadow-weaver, born to mentor Tweed and Hoffa!

[ENCELADUS emerges, fog swirling.]

ENCELADUS: Secrets are my shield, Mother—none pierce my veil!

GAIA: Mimas, vote-thief; Polybotes, land-grabber; Ephialtes, justice-twister!

[MIMAS, POLYBOTES, and EPHIALTES rise, each with a menacing gesture.]

GAIA: Pallas, crony-king; Hippolytus, tax-dodger; Gration, soul-trader!

[PALLAS, HIPPOLYTUS, and GRATION step forward, smirking.]

GAIA: Thoon & Agrius, coin-washers; Clytius, squanderer; Eurytus, poison-lord!

[THOON & AGRIUS, CLYTIUS, and EURYTUS emerge, their props—cash, files, drugs—gleaming.]

GAIA: (*Triumphant*) Go, my children, to Samaismela! A land choked by corruption, scarred by colonial chains, ripe for your reign. Sow chaos, defy Zeus, and let mortals bow!

[The GIANTS roar, scattering off-stage in all directions to quick DRUM ROLLS & CYMBALS, their laughter echoing. GAIA stands alone, her smile fierce. The NARRATOR steps forward.]

NARRATOR: (*To audience*) Samaismela trembles as the Giants descend—bribes, cartels, shadows, and worse. But the Sovereigns stir, and Olympia watches. Will justice rise, or corruption reign? Act 2 awaits, where battlefields ignite—courts, squares, and hearts. Stay sharp!

[LIGHTS FADE. CURTAINS CLOSE to a final CYMBAL CRASH, leaving the audience in anticipation.]

***

ACT 2

SCENE 1 – THE STIRRINGS OF WAR

Setting: Celestial Olympia, a resplendent garden of ethereal beauty. Gazebos with white cornices gleam under a golden sky, draped in vines and shimmering mist. Marble paths wind through lush greenery, and a crystal fountain sparkles center-stage. The 12 OLYMPIANS—ZEUS, HERA, POSEIDON, ATHENA, APOLLO, ARTEMIS, HEPHAESTUS, HERMES, DIONYSUS, ARES, DEMETER, and APHRODITE—lounge in majestic robes, their divine aura radiant. Soft LYRE MUSIC and CHIMES create a tranquil ambiance, undercut by an ominous undertone of distant DRUMS.

Characters in Scene 1:
Olympians: Zeus, Hera, Poseidon, Athena, Apollo, Artemis, Hephaestus, Hermes, Dionysus, Ares, Demeter, Aphrodite.
Narrator: Charismatic guide, engaging the audience.
Giants: Alcyoneus, Porphyrion, Enceladus, Mimas, Polybotes, Ephialtes, Pallas, Hippolytus, Gration, Thoon & Agrius, Clytius, Eurytus (appear in Scene 2).
Offstage: Gaia, Heracles (Sovereigns), Whistleblower (implied).

[Lights up. The OLYMPIANS are scattered across the garden, chatting animatedly in small groups. ATHENA and APOLLO debate strategy near a gazebo; ARTEMIS polishes her bow; DIONYSUS sips from a goblet, laughing with APHRODITE. ZEUS and HERA sit on a marble

bench, their regal presence commanding. The LYRE MUSIC hums softly. POSEIDON storms in from stage left, trident in hand, his robes damp and eyes blazing. The music falters.]

POSEIDON: (*Booming*) Olympians, hear me! A tremor shook my seas—an earthquake not of my making! Who dares meddle in my dominion? (*Points at ATHENA*) Athena, is this your scheming? Your grudge for Athens still stings, does it not?
ATHENA: (*Rising, cool and composed*) Poseidon, your floods on Athens are ancient history. I weave wisdom, not quakes. Accuse another—your temper clouds your sight.

[The OLYMPIANS murmur, intrigued. ARTEMIS steps forward, bow in hand, her expression sharp.]

ARTEMIS: (*Firmly*) Hold, Poseidon. I felt it too. Hunting under moonlight, I missed a stag—an easy shot—when the earth shuddered beneath me. (*Glances at APOLLO*) I thought Apollo's blinding light was toying with my aim, as he often does.
APOLLO: (*Laughing, strumming his harp*) Sister, my light only dazzles, not quakes! Blame your aim, not me. But this tremor... it smells of deeper mischief.

[HERMES flutters in from stage right, winged sandals gleaming. He lands lightly, then pauses, catching himself mid-sentence.]

HERMES: (Casually) I was flying back from an errand when—(Stops, smirking) Never mind.
ZEUS: (*Leaning forward, eyes narrowing*) And?
HERMES: (*Measured, glancing at HERA*) Nothing of interest. I... thought I saw Gaia slipping from Tartarus' chambers. A fleeting shadow, nothing more.

[HERA looks away, avoiding ZEUS' gaze. APOLLO steps forward, grinning slyly.]

APOLLO: (*Teasing*) Nothing of interest from Hermes always invites much interest. Remember when he, a mere toddler, stole my herd? No one thought a babe could pull it off!
ZEUS: (*Suspicious*) Where were you coming from, Hermes?
HERMES: (*Glancing at HERA, deflecting*) Oh, just... errands, mighty Zeus. (*Picks up APOLLO's harp, strumming clumsily*) Lovely tune, brother.

[HERA rises, her voice sharp, cutting through the tension.]

HERA: (*Furious*) Enough games, Hermes! Zeus, I thought your dalliance with that mortal woman taught you wisdom, but your indiscretions persist! Heracles labors in Samaismela because you couldn't restrain yourself! (*Points at the OLYMPIANS*) And mark my words—none of you aid him, or worse awaits!
APOLLO: (*Steering back*) Let's not lose the hunt. Hermes saw Gaia leave Tartarus. Do you know what that means?

[POSEIDON stomps his trident, unleashing a THUNDEROUS BOOM that shakes the stage. The OLYMPIANS startle.]

POSEIDON: (*Roaring*) She dares defy us again!
ZEUS: (*Rising, voice stern*) Watch yourself, brother. Gaia's grief is no light matter, but we are the cosmos' keepers.
POSEIDON: (*Defiant*) She wouldn't dare!
DIONYSUS: (*Lifting his goblet*) Oh, but she has. I've heard whistles in Samaismela—sharp, piercing. I thought it was my vintage, potent from Titanomachy's chaos. (*Chuckles*) Seems Gaia is brewing trouble instead.
POSEIDON: (*Clenching his trident*) This means war!

[POSEIDON storms off stage left, the stage trembling faintly. HERMES dusts his winged sandals, grinning.]

HERMES: (*Gleefully*) Great! When shall we begin?

[*The OLYMPIANS turn to ZEUS, who steps forward, his gaze piercing. He looks directly into the audience, his expression blank, heavy with foreboding. The LIGHTS DIM as the CURTAINS CLOSE to a slow DRUM ROLL.*]

[*In front of the closed curtains, a SPOTLIGHT illuminates the NARRATOR, who strides to center-stage, vibrant and conspiratorial. A faint WHISTLE blows off-stage, the Rhythm Tate-taa-taa, sharp and fleeting.*]

NARRATOR: (*To audience, with a wink*) Did you hear that?

(*The WHISTLE blows the Rhythm Tate-taa-taa*),

A whistle in Olympia's gardens, where gods bicker and tremors stir. The Titanomachy's scars run deep, and Gaia's shadow looms. In Samaismela, corruption festers—bribes, cartels, stolen lands—while the Sovereigns, our Heracles, labor on. But what have the Giants been up to? Will they make Gaia proud?

(*Pauses, leaning forward*) And that whistleblower—who are they? A citizen? A god? Keep your eyes peeled, for Samaismela's battlefields await!

(*Exits stage right, clapping the whistle's Rhythm Tate-taa-taa.*)

***

SCENE 2: THE GIANTS' PORTRAIT

[*CURTAINS OPEN. The stage transforms into a lush, open space in Samaismela, vibrant with green meadows and a backdrop of colonial-era buildings, hinting at corruption's deep roots. A large camera on a tripod stands stage left, aimed at the 12 GIANTS, posed for a group portrait. ALCYONEUS sits center in a colonial pith helmet, khaki shorts, and high socks, exuding imperial arrogance. On his left sit PORPHYRION (gold-chained suit), ENCELADUS (foggy cloak), and MIMAS (garish campaign outfit—like Stanley Ipkiss). On his right sit POLYBOTES (settler garb), EPHIALTES (stained judicial robes), and PALLAS (flashy suit). Standing behind, evenly spaced, are HIPPOLYTUS (sleek suit with offshore files), GRATION (hooded cloak with chains), THOON & AGRIUS (pinstripe suits with cash), CLYTIUS (disheveled colonial official's khaki uniform), and EURYTUS (narco-lord attire with drug caches). Gaia lurks stage left, observing.*]

ALCYONEUS: (*Rising, voice commanding*) Brothers, as we await the camera's flash, let us recount our triumphs in Samaismela. This land, scarred by colonial chains and modern greed, bends to our will. Speak, each in turn—how fares your dominion?

[*The GIANTS nod, their expressions smug. One by one, they step to the front of the stage, addressing the audience with swagger, then return to their positions. DRUMS pulse softly, building tension.*]

PORPHYRION: (*Striding forward, clutching contracts*) I, Porphyrion, weave tender cartels tighter than Rockefeller's oil empire. Samaismela's roads, hospitals—mine to rig! Like Vanderbilt's railways, my deals choke the treasury. (*Bows mockingly, retreats.*)

ENCELADUS: (*Emerging through fog, voice low*) Enceladus, I cloak Samaismela's budgets in shadow, as Tweed did New York. Audits vanish, secrets thrive—no Sovereign pierces my veil. (*Smirks, steps back.*)

MIMAS: (*Tossing fake ballots, grinning*) Mimas, vote-thief, rigs Samaismela's polls chaos. Ballots bend to my whim—elections are my stage! (*Laughs, returns.*)

POLYBOTES: (*Waving land deeds*) I, Polybotes, seize lands as British settlers did Kenya's Highlands, , Canada's prairie's, Australia's last frontier; as the Germans did Namibia's plains and as the Spanish did America and Mexico. Farms, forests—mine by right! The Sovereigns' cries amuse me. (*Sneers, steps back.*)

EPHIALTES: (*Adjusting stained robes*) Ephialtes, I twist Samaismela's courts. Judges bow to my gold, as in global scandals. Justice? A commodity I sell, because injustice begets injustice! (*Chuckles, retreats.*)

PALLAS: (*Handing out favors*) Pallas, I crown cronies—boards, contracts, all for friends. Samaismela's state and public service appointments are my playground, like patronage worldwide. (*Winks, returns.*)

HIPPOLYTUS: (*Clutching offshore files*) Hippolytus, I spirit wealth to tax havens, as in the Panama and Pandora Papers. Samaismela's taxes? Fools' burdens I evade! (*Smirks, steps back.*)

GRATION: (*Rattling chains*) Gration, I trade souls—Samaismela's desperate, trafficked to distant lands. Like global rings, I profit on pain. (*Glares, retreats.*)

THOON & AGRIUS: (*Counting cash and speaking in unison*) Thoon & Agrius, we wash Samaismela's coin clean, as Rothstein, Capone and Lansky did. Banks, havens—our empire launders all! We have our people among security agencies; they alert us to new revenue streams. (*Grin, return.*)

CLYTIUS: (*Dropping mismanaged files*) Clytius, I squander Samaismela's states, provinces and counties, as audits reveal. Budgets vanish, projects die—my legacy! (*Shrugs, steps back.*)

EURYTUS: (*Brandishing drug caches*) Eurytus, I flood Samaismela with poison, as Escobar, Kinahan and Akasha did. Streets kneel to my powder! (*Laughs darkly, retreats.*)

ALCYONEUS: (*Rising, triumphant*) Brothers, Gaia smiles! From Rhodes and Delamere's bribes to modern schemes, Samaismela is ours. Let this portrait immortalize our reign!

[The GIANTS strike a proud pose, facing the audience. The camera flashes, but a sharp WHISTLE blows off-stage, startling them. They freeze, glancing nervously. The FLASH blinds the stage as the CURTAINS CLOSE to a final DRUM BEAT.]

***

3

ACT 3

THE COSMIC CONFRONTATION

Setting: A lush, open space in Samaismela, moments after the Giants' group portrait. The stage is vibrant with green meadows, framed by colonial-era buildings that hint at entrenched corruption. The 12 GIANTS—ALCYONEUS, PORPHYRION, ENCELADUS, MIMAS, POLYBOTES, EPHIALTES, PALLAS, HIPPOLYTUS, GRATION, THOON & AGRIUS, CLYTIUS, and EURYTUS—stand frozen as statues, their poses proud and menacing, centered around ALCYONEUS in his colonial pith helmet and khaki attire. The camera from their portrait lies stage left, its flash still warm. A soft breeze carries distant DRUMS, signaling tension. The audience cannot yet see ZEUS, who lurks unseen.

Characters in Scene 1:

Zeus: Leader of the Olympians, justice's pinnacle.

Gaia: Earth Mother, elite patronage.

Heracles: The Sovereigns, global citizens.

Hades: Lord of the underworld.

Giants: Alcyoneus (bribe-takers), Porphyrion (tender cartels), Enceladus (systemic opacity), Mimas (electoral fraud), Polybotes (land grabbers), Ephialtes (judicial sabotage), Pallas (cronyism), Hippolytus (tax evasion), Gration (human trafficking), Thoon & Agrius (money laundering), Clytius (state & county mismanagement), Eurytus (drug lords).

ACT 3

Narrator: Charismatic guide, engaging the audience.
Offstage: Other Olympians, Whistleblower (implied).

[Lights up. The GIANTS remain statue-like, their expressions smug. GAIA enters stage right, prancing in a solo waltz, her earthy robes flowing like roots. Her movements are graceful yet defiant, a silent celebration of her Giants' triumphs. The DRUMS pulse softly, underscored by a haunting FLUTE melody. GAIA senses a presence, pausing mid-waltz as she crosses to stage left.]

GAIA: (*Smirking, without turning*) What can I do for you, Zeus? I am not one of your dames.

[ZEUS emerges from stage right, stepping from behind GAIA's path. His celestial robes shimmer, lightning crackling faintly in his hand. GAIA continues her waltz to center-stage, then stops, posing confidently with arms crossed across her chest. The FLUTE fades, leaving only DRUMS.]

ZEUS: (*Voice stern, measured*) You have crossed the line this time, Gaia. I thought we had put war behind us, settled order in the cosmos.
GAIA: (*Laughing bitterly*) You Olympians crossed the line, Zeus! Casting my Titans into Tartarus—my children, my blood!
ZEUS: (*Stepping closer*) How did we? You are our grandmother. You were meant to shield us from Cronus, not aid his tyranny.
GAIA: (*Eyes blazing*) Cronus was my liberator! He freed me from Uranus' oppression, that tyrant you call a god!
ZEUS: (*Firmly*) You chose Uranus, Gaia. Why should we suffer for your decisions? Cronus devoured us—your grandchildren—to cling to power.
GAIA: (*Defiant*) He kept you safe within the universe's womb! There was cosmic order then, a harmony you shattered!

ZEUS: (*Voice rising*) Shackles do not make order. Free will, freedom—these are divine rights. You, of all celestial beings, should know this!

GAIA: (*Yelling, fists clenched*) And so you overthrew your father and chained him in Tartarus! What justice is that?

ZEUS: (*Calm but resolute*) Better than Cronus' crime—castrating his own father. I stand to break this cycle, Gaia. I stand for cohesion, truth, justice. War begets war.

GAIA: (*Sneering*) Justice? Casting my Titans beneath Hades' underworld is more than any mother can bear! You call that cohesion?

ZEUS: (*Softly, pained*) You know Hades holds mortal souls, Gaia. The Titans had none—they were chaos incarnate.

GAIA: (*Furious*) And who anointed you judge over the cosmos? You, a usurper, dare lecture me?

[GAIA spins, her robes swirling, and storms off stage left, her laughter echoing. The DRUMS intensify. HERACLES enters stage left, brushing past GAIA. He pauses, surprised, then locks eyes with ZEUS. HERACLES, rugged and weary, carries a bow and quiver, embodying the Sovereigns' resilience.]

HERACLES: (*Wryly*) Man is born free, but everywhere he is in chains. I suppose the mighty Zeus wouldn't grasp this mortal philosophy.

ZEUS: (Forlorn, haggard) But I do, Heracles.

[HERACLES sits on a log stage center, tightening his bowstring with deliberate care. The DRUMS soften to a heartbeat rhythm: Tate-Ta, Tate Ta.]

HERACLES: (*Glancing up*) Yet here we are—you, the mightiest celestial, and I, a mere mortal, pondering the next seconds of our tangled paths.

ZEUS: (*Quietly*) Heracles, I am your father.

HERACLES: (*Firmly*) No, you are not.

ZEUS: (*Pleading*) As hard as it is to face, I am.

HERACLES: (*Pensively, tightening bow*) Children cling to fathers for sustenance, protection. When those needs fade, the father is freed from duty, and children from obedience. (*Pauses, testing the bow*) You owe me nothing, Zeus.

ZEUS: (*Stepping closer*) Your wisdom has grown, Heracles. It will serve you well. Strength alone never masters forever—not unless it bends to a just cause, and obedience upholds duty. Might carves rights, but free will binds us to legitimate powers.

HERACLES: (*Standing, resolute*) As a man of free will, I choose to wield it, even against celestial whims. Free will levels us—no god above, no mortal below.

[HERACLES shoulders his bow and exits stage right, brushing past HADES, who enters hauling a fishing net brimming with glowing souls. HADES, cloaked in dark robes, sets his load center-stage. ZEUS approaches, his expression troubled.]

HADES: (*Gruffly, adjusting net*) Greetings, brother. What trouble now? Rumblings above my dominion warn of a soul-haul too vast for my gates.

ZEUS: (*Earnestly*) Hades, in your time below, have you found a way to share souls with those in Tartarus?

HADES: (*Lifting his net, scoffing*) No, Zeus, and I won't. Tartarus is irredeemable—its acid burns all who enter. Don't tempt that abyss, brother. (*Exits stage left, dragging his net, souls flickering.*)

[ZEUS turns to the GIANTS, who begin to stir, their statue-like poses breaking into quiet murmurs, inaudible to the audience. ZEUS approaches ALCYONEUS, motioning for a private word. They move to the

front of center-stage, the other GIANTS watching slyly. The DRUMS pulse ominously.]

ALCYONEUS: (*Smirking, in colonial pith helmet*) That mighty Zeus seeks my ear speaks of victory near. What words, Olympian?
ZEUS: (*Steadily*) That I seek words means redemption lies within your free will, Alcyoneus. Do not squander it.
ALCYONEUS: (*Laughing*) Redemption? You preach cohesion, truth, justice, yet Samaismela thrives on our chaos! It's time, Zeus, to yield to the Giants—forged in Tartarus' fire by Gaia's vengeance. Your Olympian strikes cannot touch us.

[ALCYONEUS steps closer, his voice dripping with historical bravado.]

ALCYONEUS: Persons of good intention rarely have the courage of solidarity. Mortals like Martin Luther, Malcolm X, Barbara Castle, Dennis Pritt, the Mau Mau, Maximillien de Robespierre, Emile Zola, Dedan Kimathi, Wangari Maathai—champions of justice, all fallen before us. The suffragettes marched, but we observed who they put at the rear. Eastern sages preached non-violence; Europe bars "undesirables" while plundering afar. Slavery ended, apartheid crumbled—yet we've woven subtler chains. Not by war, Zeus, but by curating the free will you exalt. Our tendrils grip every cosmos' corner. We provided disruptions to your cosmic order. Free will, unexercised, bows to our relentless disruptions. Samaismela's mortals kneel to us, and if you Olympians deny it—prepare for war!
ZEUS: (*Voice like thunder*) Well then, so be it. Prepare for war!
ALCYONEUS: (*Triumphant*) War it is! Come, brothers!

[The GIANTS roar, their serpentine legs coiling as they march off stage left, ALCYONEUS leading with a mocking salute. ZEUS exits stage right, his face grim. TRUMPETS OF WAR blare, fierce and resolute.

The CURTAINS CLOSE to a crescendo of DRUMS: Tate taa-Tate taa-Tate taa.]

[In front of the closed curtains, a SPOTLIGHT bathes the NARRATOR, who strides to center-stage, vibrant and philosophical. The air hums with tension.]

NARRATOR: (*To audience, with gravitas*) War looms, as Zeus and Gaia clash, their words a cosmic duel of free will and vengeance. Heracles, the Sovereigns' heart, claims equality with gods, while Hades guards his souls from Tartarus' maw. Alcyoneus, bold and unyielding, boasts of Giants' dominion—from colonial bribes to modern schemes.
(Pauses, leaning forward)
A prophecy whispers: only a mortal can fell these Giants. But who? Martin Luther? Wangari Maathai? Or another yet unseen?
(Points to audience)
Name a mortal, you who watch—who carries Heracles' bow today? And that whistleblower—did they stir this war's trumpets? (*Smiles slyly*) Samaismela's battlefields await—courts, squares, hearts. Stay sharp!

[The NARRATOR exits stage right, humming a faint whistle. The stage darkens, leaving the audience pondering.]

***

ACT 4

SCENE 1 – THE COURTROOM CLASH

Setting: A grand courtroom in Samaismela, steeped in colonial echoes yet vibrant with modern tension. A high judge's bench looms center-stage, flanked by a gavel and scales of justice.

On the right, the 12 OLYMPIANS—ZEUS, HERA, POSEIDON, ATHENA, APOLLO, ARTEMIS, HEPHAESTUS, HERMES, DIONYSUS, ARES, DEMETER, APHRODITE—stand in celestial robes, their expressions resolute.

On the left, the 12 GIANTS—ALCYONEUS, PORPHYRION, ENCELADUS, MIMAS, POLYBOTES, EPHIALTES, PALLAS, HIPPOLYTUS, GRATION, THOON & AGRIUS, CLYTIUS, EURYTUS—sit smugly, their costumes (pith helmet, gold chains, foggy cloak, etc.) exuding corruption.

GAIA lingers behind the Giants, her earthy robes blending into the shadows. The audience, representing Samaismela's Sovereigns, fills the background. PULSATING DRUMS underscore the scene, punctuated by a faint WHISTLE off-stage.

Characters in Scene 1:
Zeus: Justice's pinnacle.
Alcyoneus: Bribe-takers, colonial leader.
Ephialtes: Judicial sabotage.
Gaia: Elite patronage.

Athena: Judiciary.
Enceladus: Systemic opacity.
Other Olympians and Giants: Silent but reactive.
Narrator: Guide, engaging the audience.
Offstage: Heracles (Sovereigns), Whistleblower (implied).

[Lights up. The courtroom buzzes with murmurs. ZEUS steps forward, lightning crackling faintly in his hand, addressing the JUDGE, a stern figure in black robes.]

ZEUS: (*Voice booming*) Your Honor, Samaismela weeps under the Giants' yoke. They usurp native rights, forging treachery in treaties—Maasai, San, Khoikhoi, Cherokee, Seminoles, Aboriginals, Navajo, all driven from their lands! Trails of Tears, Caravans of Sorrow, scorched earth policies—Alcyoneus' incited the declaration, "Kill every buffalo you can; every buffalo dead is an Indian gone!" Justice demands their reckoning!

[The OLYMPIANS nod gravely. The GIANTS smirk, ALCYONEUS rising with imperial swagger, his pith helmet gleaming.]

ALCYONEUS: (*Smoothly*) Zeus, you paint us villains, but colonization civilized Samaismela! From tribal feuds to railroads and cities, we brought progress. Rhodes' mines, Delamere's ranches, the Belle Grove Plantation, the OVC or as it is popularly known, the Dutch East India Company —advancements born of dominion. Without us, this land would languish in chaos.

ZEUS: (*Fierce*) Progress? You colonists were a law unto yourselves, unaccountable to your nations as you wrought atrocities from the Pacific and Atlantic to Africa! No oversight, no justice—only plunder. (*Pauses, to the JUDGE*) I pose this: should descendants of these colonizers bear their ancestors' guilt?

[ALCYONEUS leaps up, voice sharp.]

ALCYONEUS: Objection! Each generation answers for its own deeds, not the past's shadows. To chain descendants to history is to shackle progress itself!

[GAIA leans toward ALCYONEUS, her voice a hushed warning.]

GAIA: (*Whispering*) Beware, Alcyoneus. A defensive argument may win here but lose the Sovereigns' favor. Legal victories fade without public goodwill.

ALCYONEUS: *(Nodding, to the JUDGE)* Gold greases empires, Your Honor. Ranches, mines—all built on sweet deals. Samaismela thrives because of us.

[ALCYONEUS nods at EPHIALTES, who rises, his judicial robes stained with gold dust. EPHIALTES approaches the JUDGE, turning his back to the OLYMPIANS. He opens his robe, revealing a pouch, and taps it, producing a JINGLING sound. He smirks and returns to his seat. The JUDGE's eyes narrow.]

ZEUS: (*Rising, indignant*) Your Honor, the Giants' bribes taint this court! Their land grabs—

[The JUDGE slams the gavel, silencing ZEUS. Murmurs ripple through the courtroom.]

JUDGE: (*Coldly*) The petitioner has not proved his case. This matter is dismissed.

[The OLYMPIANS gasp, the GIANTS chuckle. The courtroom erupts in MURMURS. The NARRATOR strides to center-stage, spotlighted, as the OLYMPIANS and GIANTS begin exiting to their respective stage sides—right for Olympians, left for Giants.]

NARRATOR: (*To audience, with a wry smile*) Was that the outcome you anticipated? A courtroom swayed by jingles, not justice. You're in for more surprises, friends—this was a barren draw. (*Pauses*) But the war rages on. Who's that whistleblower, stirring the air? Keep watching!

[A RING-SIDE BELL rings sharply. As the GIANTS and OLYMPIANS exit, ATHENA intercepts ENCELADUS, blocking his path stage left. Her aegis gleams, her voice sharp.]

ATHENA: (*Accusing*) Enceladus, we know you seized Rothstein's file cabinets from his Fifth Avenue lair—proof of his narcotics ring and slot machine rackets. We know of your $100-per-plate Copacabana dinner, wining corrupt judges. Have you no shred of transparency?

ENCELADUS: (Smirking, fog swirling) Transparency? Tweed's New York thrived in shadows, Athena. Opacity saves mankind from itself. Transparent systems remain an aspiration but they cannot stand the nakedness of truth. Samaismela's too far gone for your light.

ATHENA: (*Shouting, pointing*) Enceladus, transparency is my shield! I will bury you in a mountain of evidence!

[ENCELADUS laughs darkly and exits stage left. ATHENA follows, her aegis raised. A RING-SIDE BELL rings again. The NARRATOR reappears, crossing from stage left to right as the CURTAINS CLOSE left to right, accompanied by PULSATING DRUMS: Tate-Taa-ta X4.]

NARRATOR: (*To audience*) Enceladus falls, true to Athena's vow, trapped under evidence's weight, rumbling like his mythic kin beneath Etna. One Giant down—but more lurk in Samaismela's shadows. Who's next? And where's that whistleblower?

***

ACT 4 — | 49 |

SCENE 2: THE BALLOT FRAUD

Setting: A desolate warehouse in Samaismela, dimly lit with flickering bulbs. Black ballot boxes are stacked haphazardly, papers spilling out. The CURTAINS are partly drawn (quarter-way) on the left, focusing light on one corner where MIMAS sits at a dark table, frantically tapping a laptop. The air is thick with deceit. A faint WHISTLE blows off-stage "Tate Taa Taa", sharp and accusing.

Characters in Scene 2:
Mimas: Electoral fraud.
Hephaestus: Institutional reform.
Narrator: Guide.

[Lights up on MIMAS, his garish campaign outfit clashing with the grim setting. He grabs papers, scans them, and tosses them aside, muttering. The WHISTLE blows again, louder "Tate Taa Taa". MIMAS freezes, then opens a ballot box, stuffing in forged papers.]

MIMAS: (*Muttering*) Votes bend to my will—Samaismela's polls are clay...

[The CURTAINS open halfway, revealing HEPHAESTUS, towering with a smith's hammer, anvil, and tongs. A distant HAMMER ON ANVIL rings intermittently.]

HEPHAESTUS: (*Voice like iron*) What is the meaning of this, Mimas?

MIMAS: (*Smirking, rising*) Votes are clay, Hephaestus—I mold them to serve! While you hammered in Olympia's forge, I shaped Samaismela's elections. What you see me tossing out are the so called Spolit votes, one of my genius moves. I didn't think it would work but it has.

(*Confidently*) You see Hephaestus, thousands of voters go to the polls angry and vow not to vote for any of the candidates we put forward. They end up crossing out all the candidates on the ballot in protest. Those votes don't count! The Electoral Commission bins them as spoilt votes and the courts hold the logic that they count towards neither candidate and thus should not form part of the total votes cast. Voila! The percentage turnout is altered and my candidates sail through.

The Electorate are mere arm-chair critics. They passively dedicate a day to my pre-determined molds. I fashion the outcomes. Have you ever seen anyone criticize clay until it turns to formed mold? No Hephaestus, one must put their hands in the potter's wheel. The Electorate's arm chair critic is akin to remodelling cast clay destined for the kiln. Fait accompli! This flaw in the electorate is more bane than boon, but they are none the wiser. Election chaos? My masterpiece!

HEPHAESTUS: (Stepping forward, hammer raised) Then it ends today Mimas, my systems will purify your fraud!

[The stage goes DARK. DRUM ROLLS crescendo, punctuated by LOUD HAMMER STRIKES on an anvil, then silence. The CURTAINS CLOSE fully.]

[A STAGE LIGHT reveals the NARRATOR in front of the curtains, voice triumphant.]

NARRATOR: Two down! Mimas, vote-thief, crushed by Hephaestus' forge. Samaismela's ballots breathe freer—but the Giants' shadow lingers. Who's the whistleblower, tipping the scales? Keep guessing!

***

SCENE 3: THE LAND DISPUTE

Setting: A rocky high ground in Samaismela, overlooking stolen communal lands. The CURTAINS open halfway on the right, revealing POSEIDON atop a cliff, trident gleaming, facing POLYBOTES below, who clutches land deeds. The backdrop shows plundered fields, echoing colonial scars. DRUMS roll, then stop abruptly, followed by a WHISTLE *"Tate Taa taa"*, CYMBALS and THUNDER.

Characters in Scene 3:
Poseidon: Legislative might.

Polybotes: Land grabbers.
Narrator: Guide.

POLYBOTES: (*Defiant, waving deeds*) These lands were empty before us, Poseidon—ask the settlers of Kanata, the white highlands and the land down under!

POSEIDON: (*Stern*) Empty communal lands are seasonal, Polybotes. Did you think the Maasai, Cherokee, or Navajo wouldn't return?

POLYBOTES: (*Sneering*) Finders keepers, Poseidon. Scramble and partition—it's the cosmic order! Ordinances and maxim guns; Explorers and missionaries. Consent can be manufactured. Land Commissions are legal instruments, participation is voluntary. These lands were signed away through deeds and do not offend established laws.

POSEIDON: (*Sarcastically*) Really? Why haven't you claimed my seas? I've waited eons for your boldness.

[DRUMS roll, then stop with CYMBALS and THUNDER. The CURTAINS CLOSE. The NARRATOR appears center-stage in front of the curtains.]

NARRATOR: Three down! Polybotes, land-grabber, drowned by Poseidon's truth. Samaismela's soils stir with hope. But the war rages—who's next? And that whistleblower... are they among us?

***

SCENE 4: THE TAX HAVEN CHASE

Setting: A shadowy Samaismela dock, littered with crates and sealed packages. The CURTAINS open halfway on the left, revealing HIPPOLYTUS sealing a package for shipment, his sleek suit gleaming with offshore wealth. A SHADOWY FIGURE looms stage left, silent and ominous. DRUMS roll softly, building suspense then the rhythm *"Tate Taa taa"* once then silence.

Characters in Scene 4:

Hippolytus: Tax evasion.

Hermes: ANTI-CORRUPTION CZAR's cunning (disguised as Hades).

Narrator: Guide.

HIPPOLYTUS: (*Smirking, to the SHADOWY FIGURE*) Aha, Hades. Here to collect souls? Hold your horses—lend a hand instead of idling.

[The SHADOWY FIGURE remains still. HIPPOLYTUS continues, patting the package.]

HIPPOLYTUS: Wondering how wealth moves, Hades? Pandora Papers, Panama Papers—just scraps journalists unearthed. Tax havens built the richest nations' fortunes. Taxes are for fools—my gold sails to Caymans, Swiss accounts, Jersey, Guernsey. (*Finalizes sealing, grins*) Done!

[DRUMS roll "Tate Taa taa" X2, stop with CYMBALS. The SHADOWY FIGURE steps into light, revealing HERMES, winged sandals gleaming, Hades' helm discarded.]

HIPPOLYTUS: (*Shocked*) Hermes! I should've known—Hades has no dress sense!

[HIPPOLYTUS dashes off stage right. HERMES dusts his sandals, grins, and gives chase. The CURTAINS CLOSE. The NARRATOR appears center-stage, spotlighted.]

NARRATOR: Four down! Hippolytus, tax-dodger, outrun by Hermes' cunning. Samaismela's wealth inches toward justice. We're entering an exciting phase in this war, friends!

(*Leans forward*)

Who's the whistleblower, blowing chaos into the Giants' schemes? Guess wisely—the battlefields burn brighter!

[The NARRATOR exits stage right, humming the whistle's tune. The stage darkens, DRUMS pulsing in suspense.]

***

SCENE 5 – THE NAKEDNESS OF TRUTH

Setting: A lush, vibrant landscape in Samaismela, a tapestry of rolling meadows, towering sequoia, and shimmering streams, symbolizing the nation's potential for renewal. The stage pulses with life, yet a shadow looms—a gaping, smoky pit representing Tartarus, positioned stage center, its edges flickering with eerie light. The air hums with PULSATING DRUMS *"Tate Taa taa" X2*, evoking both hope and impending judgment. HERACLES, embodying the Sovereigns, stands stage left, bow in hand, surrounded by a chorus of diverse citizens (farmers, students, workers) wielding placards and smartphones. The 12 OLYMPIANS and remaining GIANTS—PORPHYRION, EPHIALTES, and CLYTIUS—await their cues, their costumes vivid against the verdant backdrop. A faint WHISTLE echoes off-stage, sharp and accusing.

Characters in Scene 5:
Heracles: The Sovereigns, global citizens.
Zeus: Justice's pinnacle.
Apollo: Truth's light.
Hecate: Adapted as Demeter's ally (replacing mythic Hecate for narrative fit).
Porphyrion: Tender cartels.
Ephialtes: Judicial sabotage.
Clytius: State & county mismanagement.
Narrator: Guide, engaging the audience.
Offstage: Gaia, other Olympians, other Giants, Whistleblower (implied).

[Lights up. The landscape glows under a golden sun, but Tartarus' pit casts a dark contrast. HERACLES steps forward, his rugged form radiant with resolve. The SOVEREIGNS' hum "Tate Taa taa" X2 flanks him. HERACLES raises his bow, addressing the audience as he begins

"The Nakedness of Truth," his voice resonant, weaving mythic poetry with Samaismela's struggle. As he performs, symbolic slayings unfold, each Giant ushered to Tartarus in a metaphorical dance of justice.]

HERACLES: (*To audience, with gravitas*)
When Truth and Lie meet today,
Ah! A good day since yesterday,
Truth looks up and confesses the splendours of the day,
Truth and Lie in privacy, in fantasy, in fancy, playfully expending mid-day.

[ZEUS enters stage right, lightning crackling, joining HERACLES. PORPHYRION, in his gold-chained suit, struts stage left, sealing a tender deal with a shadowy figure. ZEUS and HERACLES march in ANIMATED HUNTING STEPS, synchronized and fierce, circling PORPHYRION. The SOVEREIGNS' clap "Tate Taa taa" X2 as a placard reads "END CARTELS."]

HERACLES:
Lie coaxing Truth, sweet waters these be, come let's take a swim,
Make no worry for your clothing, here, let's indulge in whim,

[ZEUS unleashes a VOLLEY OF THUNDERBOLTS—bright flashes of light—striking PORPHYRION, who staggers. HERACLES looses a STRING OF ARROWS, symbolic beams piercing PORPHYRION's contracts. The SOVEREIGNS' clap "Tate Taa taa" X2 as PORPHYRION is dragged by ZEUS and HERACLES to Tartarus' pit, where he vanishes with a wail. The DRUMS pulse faster "Ta Ta Ta (1 second pause then...) Tate taa taa" X2.]

HERACLES:
Truth never shilly-shallying, sashaying and prancing, to the waters so gleam,
To ponder, on yonder, observing pleasure in maxim.

[APOLLO *enters stage right, his harp glowing, moving* BACK-TO-BACK *with* HERACLES *in* ANIMATED DRAMA. EPHIALTES, *in stained judicial robes, sneers stage left, clutching a bribe-filled pouch. The* SOVEREIGNS' *hum "Tate-taa-taa" as they wave smartphones, recording* EPHIALTES' *treachery while the two move.* APOLLO *and* HERACLES *shoot* ARROWS *in unison, covering each other, their movements a choreographed dance of precision.*]

HERACLES:
In spiff whiff, Lie egressing whence the waters,
Saunters ditzy skiffy, to the palming trees, potters, genteel mannerism falters,

[EPHIALTES *dodges, but the arrows—beams of light—strike true, exposing his corruption. The* DRUMS *beat "Ta Ta Ta (1 second pause then...) Tate taa taa" X2.* EPHIALTES *stumbles, clutching his robes, and is ushered by* APOLLO *and* HERACLES *to Tartarus' pit, vanishing with a defiant cry. A* WHISTLE *blows off-stage once, sharp and triumphant Tate-taa-taa"*]

HERACLES:
Donning Truth's clothes, stock-still in the waters,
Speeding off, raising dust, tutelary spirit totters.

[HECATE, *adapted as* DEMETER's *ally, enters stage right, her torches blazing, symbolizing equity's light. She joins* HERACLES, *and they* DRAMATICALLY SURROUND CLYTIUS, *who stands stage left in a disheveled colonial official's uniform, dropping mismanaged files. The* SOVEREIGNS' *clap "Tate Taa taa" X2, as a placard reads "States serve!"* HECATE's *torches cast flickering shadows, trapping* CLYTIUS *in a circle of light.*]

HERACLES:

In panic disco, Truth materializing, uncapricious, from the waters seething,
Giving chase, steaming, in just cause, impatience teeming,

[CLYTIUS panics, flinging files, but HECATE's torches flare, and HERACLES' arrows—symbolic beams—pin him. The DRUMS beat "Ta Ta Ta (1 second pause then...) Tate taa taa" X2 CLYTIUS collapses, and HECATE and HERACLES usher him to Tartarus' pit, where he vanishes with a whimper. The SOVEREIGNS' clap "Tate Taa taa" X2.]

HERACLES:

Discord alas! Mankind seeing Truth unseeming,
Mockery, derision, ostracizing Truth; to the ponds, to the wells, whence efflorescing.

[HERACLES steps center-stage, the SOVEREIGNS' encircling him, their placards. Tartarus' pit glows faintly, its hunger sated for now.]

HERACLES:

On this day, Lie is with us, welcomed with open arms,
Sartorial Lie beguiles Truth, true-lies in open swarms,
Because fellow humans eschew Truth blatantly,
And shun the Nakedness of Truth flagrantly.

[HERACLES lowers his bow, gazing at the audience. The SOVEREIGNS raise their smartphones, recording the moment, a nod to modern activism. A final WHISTLE blows, louder "Tate Taa taa", as the LIGHTS DIM. The CURTAINS CLOSE to a slow DRUM ROLL "Ta Ta Ta (1 second pause then...) Tate taa taa", leaving Tartarus' pit faintly visible.]

[A SPOTLIGHT illuminates the NARRATOR, who strides to center-stage in front of the closed curtains, vibrant and reflective.]

NARRATOR: (*To audience, with a knowing grin*) Seven down! Porphyrion's cartels, Ephialtes' bribes, Clytius' waste—felled by Truth's naked glare, ushered to Tartarus' jaws. Heracles, Samaismela's Sovereigns, wields poetry and power, joined by Zeus, Apollo, and Hecate.

(Pauses, leaning forward)

But Lies still swarm, as the poem warns. Who's the whistleblower, piercing these Giants' schemes? And who's the mortal of prophecy, destined to end this war?

(Points to audience) Name a hero—past or present—who carries Truth's bow? The battlefields burn hotter, friends—stay sharp!

[The NARRATOR exits stage right, humming the whistle's tune. The stage darkens, DRUMS pulsing in suspense.]

***

ACT 5

SCENE 1 – THE PLENARY COURT OF OLYMPIA

Setting: The curtains are closed. A SPOTLIGHT illuminates the NARRATOR, standing stage right in front of the curtains, their presence commanding and reflective. The air hums with anticipation, underscored by soft, PULSATING DRUMS. The stage is poised for a cosmic reckoning.

Characters in Scene 1:
Narrator: Charismatic guide, engaging the audience.
Heracles: The Sovereigns, global citizens.
Olympians: Zeus, Hera, Athena, Hermes, Ares (others implied).
Offstage: Artemis, Dionysus, The Moirai (Fates), Giants, Gaia, Whistleblower (implied).

[Lights up on the NARRATOR, spotlighted, addressing the audience with fervor.]

NARRATOR: (*To audience, with gravitas*) To minimize or to eradicate? Idealists chase the latter, hearts ablaze with dreams of a cleansed cosmos. Skeptics cling to the former, cloaking complacency in cries of "Let's be realistic!" Why speak for realists? Because eradication is grueling, not a single blow but a relentless march—effort skeptics shun. They scorn idealists, for trauma has taught them to cradle mediocrity, a paradigm idealists dare to shatter.

(*Pauses, turning right, voice rising*) OOOOOOLYMPIANS, Heracles wishes to address you!

[*As the NARRATOR shouts, the CURTAINS OPEN, revealing the plenary court of Olympia, a celestial chamber of marble columns and golden light. The 12 OLYMPIANS sit in a semicircle, their robes shimmering, faces pensive. ZEUS presides on a throne, lightning in hand. HERA, ATHENA, HERMES, and ARES are prominent, others implied. HERACLES stands stage right at the gates, rugged yet radiant, bow slung across his back, embodying the Sovereigns' resolve. DRUMS soften to a heartbeat rhythm.*]

HERA: (*Surprised, rising*) How did he make it here?
ARES: (*Grinning*) He's braved Uncle Hades' underworld and returned. Olympia's gates are no barrier.
ATHENA: (*Nodding*) He completed his Twelve Labors.
HERMES: (*Smirking, dusting winged sandals*) Thirteen, Athena, thirteen.

[*The OLYMPIANS turn to HERMES, eyebrows raised.*]

HERMES: (*Waving dismissively*) There is the matter of King Thespius' fifty daughters... (Flicks hand) Well, never mind.
ZEUS: (*Authoritative*) I decree Heracles has completed his labors.
HERA: (*Protesting*) It's not for you to—

[*A FLASH OF LIGHTNING illuminates the court, followed by THUNDER. The OLYMPIANS fall silent. HERA glares but sits.*]

ZEUS: (*To HERA*) Have you forgotten who rescued us from Porphyrion? Technically, he's still mortal—that's why he stands at Olympia's gates. (*Turning to HERACLES*) Speak, Heracles.

HERACLES: (*Stepping forward, voice resolute*) I wish to end the Gigantomachy.

[*The OLYMPIANS arch their necks, murmuring in surprise.*]

ZEUS: (*Skeptical*) And how, exactly, do you intend to achieve that? The remaining Giants—Alcyoneus, Pallas, Gration, Thoon & Agrius, Eurytus—are formidable, even against Olympian might.
HERACLES: (*Firmly*) I reserve the details to myself and the final executors, lest celestial rivalries disrupt the outcome.
ZEUS: (*Pensively, rising and pacing*) Very well, Heracles. You've earned this. What do you need?
HERACLES: (*With conviction*) I need Artemis, Dionysus, Athena, and The Moirai.

[*The OLYMPIANS exchange glances, nodding slowly. ZEUS raises his hand, sealing the decree. The DRUMS crescendo, then stop. The CURTAINS CLOSE.*]

***

SCENE 2 – THE PUBLIC SQUARE OF SAMAISMELA

Setting: A sunny public square in a modern Samaismela city, radiating hope and renewal. Clean streets gleam under a bright sky, lined with sleek buildings symbolizing potential. The crowd—SOVEREIGNS in diverse, modern attire (suits, athletic gear, workmen's clothes, doctors' gowns, lawyers' robes, school uniforms)—mills about, vibrant and engaged.

Stage left, the remaining GIANTS—ALCYONEUS (pith helmet), PALLAS (flashy suit), GRATION (hooded cloak), THOON &

ACT 5 — | 61 |

AGRIUS (pinstripe suits), EURYTUS (narco-lord attire)—converse smugly.

Stage right, HERACLES enters, followed by ARTEMIS (bow gleaming), DIONYSUS (goblet raised), ATHENA (aegis shining), and THE MOIRAI (three cloaked figures, threads in hand).

TARTARUS, a dark haze like a paper kite, lurks off-stage, ready to strike. PULSATING DRUMS and CHORAL CLAPS set a triumphant tone, punctuated by a faint WHISTLE off-stage.

Characters in Scene 2:
Heracles: The Sovereigns, global citizens.
Artemis: Civic purity.
Dionysus: Youthful zeal.
Athena: Judiciary.
The Moirai: Fates, cosmic justice.
Alcyoneus: Bribe-takers.
Pallas: Cronyism.
Gration: Human trafficking.
Thoon & Agrius: Money laundering.
Eurytus: Drug lords.
Sovereigns: Chorus of citizens.
Offstage: Tartarus, Zeus, Gaia, Whistleblower (implied).

[Lights up. The SOVEREIGNS mingle, their chatter lively. The GIANTS, stage left, whisper confidently. HERACLES strides to stage center, chanting rhythmically, his voice a clarion call.]

HERACLES: (*Chanting*) Oh land o' lilies! Oh land o' lilies! Oh land o' lilies!

[ARTEMIS, DIONYSUS, ATHENA, and THE MOIRAI follow, halting a short distance behind. The SOVEREIGNS turn, drawn to HERACLES. The GIANTS glance over, intrigued.]

ALCYONEUS: (*To Giants, smirking*) What's the son of Zeus up to? Let's get close and listen.

[The GIANTS move slightly toward center-stage, wary but mocking. THE MOIRAI discreetly encircle THOON & AGRIUS (Thoon & Agrius's mythic twin, adapted here), separating them from the others. TARTARUS appears stage left, a dark haze, and swallows THOON & AGRIUS silently, then vanishes. The other GIANTS, unaware, focus on HERACLES.]

HERACLES: (*Softly, then crescendoing*) Sovereigns of Samaismela! Oh SOVEREIGNS OF SAMAISMELA! I have news for you!

[The SOVEREIGNS gather closer, cheering. The GIANTS laugh loudly, ALCYONEUS stepping forward.]

ALCYONEUS: (*Hysterically*) Indulge us, oh son of Zeus!

[The GIANTS join in laughter, dispersing to various corners of the square, halting to watch HERACLES mockingly. HERACLES, undeterred, lifts his bow, stringing an arrow, locking eyes with DIONYSUS, who raises his goblet in acknowledgment.]

HERACLES: (*Resolute*) I will honor your indulgence.

[HERACLES begins reciting "Oh Land o' Lilies," a poem of reclaiming heritage and overcoming plunder, his voice soaring. The SOVEREIGNS sway, inspired. Each stanza cues a Giant's fall, choreographed

ACT 5 — | 63 |

with Olympian precision, aligning the poem's imagery with Samaismela's anti-corruption fight.]

> **HERACLES**: (Stanza 1)
> In the land on yonder, in wander and wonder,
> The caravans slow ponder, a heritage of plunder,
> Bequeath ne'er new bequest under,
> Dwell ye in spirit of the land sander.

[DIONYSUS moves toward EURYTUS, stage right, his thyrsus glowing. He dances, rallying SOVEREIGNS with anti-drug chants—"No more poison!" EURYTUS, clutching drug caches, sneers but falters as DIONYSUS' zeal, echoing global drug busts, overwhelms him. TARTARUS appears stage right, swallowing EURYTUS with a wail, then exits. The SOVEREIGNS cheer, DRUMS pulsing, a WHISTLE piercing the air.]

> **HERACLES**: (Stanza 2)
> Sorrow westerly pitter-patter,
> For the land hinter-hunter,
> Any shin ne'er be, in you wit may tea-totter,
> Welcoming, easterly shores pity-pat 'er.

[ATHENA glides toward PALLAS, stage left, her aegis raised. She confronts PALLAS, who stumbles. TARTARUS appears stage left, swallowing PALLAS with a cry, then exits. THE SAMAISMELA SHIELD appears and ATHENA displays it in victory, DRUMS intensifying.]

> **HERACLES**: (Stanza 3)
> Nations build fast, first billed nay shone,
> Shay hone, lay tone, shea norm, bey gone,
> Pledge fealty, make known, a heritage unknown,
> Reclaiming renown, for generations in awn.

[ARTEMIS stalks toward GRATION, stage right, her bow drawn. GRATION, rattling chains, recoils as ARTEMIS' arrows—beams of light—strike. TARTARUS appears stage right, swallowing GRATION with a snarl, then exits. The SOVEREIGNS ululate, DRUMS crescendoing "Tate Taa taa".]

[HERACLES finishes the poem, lowering his bow. The SOVEREIGNS encircle him, placards reading "SOVEREIGNTY NOW." ALCYONEUS, alone, strides to center-stage, facing HERACLES. ARTEMIS, DIONYSUS, ATHENA, and THE MOIRAI exit stage right, their work done.]

ALCYONEUS: (*Coldly*) It is obvious that fate is on your side and Tartarus is a fate to be embraced. Before either of us makes that journey, there are some truths we must cast in spell.

[ALCYONEUS moves to the fore of the stage, addressing the audience, his pith helmet gleaming.]

You see, Heracles. While you rely on the collective goodwill of these people, we the giants, are guaranteed of their individual greed, jealousy and impulsiveness; *(pointing randomly left, right and center of the audience)* from that one, that one and this one.

(*Still looking at the audience*) You may have robbed me the company of my fellow Giants in this epic encounter but the centuries of our reach cannot be brought down in a singular event. The more the people multiply, the more their greed for land grows. Polybotes lives on. The more the government tenders they develop, the more Porphyrion is exalted, the more Enceladus legacy lives on.

We did not create cartels; they did (*pointing at the audience*). They created cartels in business and called them Business communities. They created cartels in politics and called them political parties. They desire efficient working government systems but they want politicians to do it for them. All we did is encourage them to believe that politics is a waste of their time and that it is a vile topic that will send them straight to Tartarus.

They know not the difference between politics and civic duty. They know not the difference between a politician and a leader. The more complacent they get with their democratic and constitutional duties, the more Mimas shadow looms.

(*Pointing at the audience*)These people only care for justice when it involves them at a personal level. They have tried Truth Justice and Reconciliation Commissions but resist the truth when it stares them in the face from the resultant reports. They prefer political correctness than the sting of truth, which they prefer to bury in farms, golf courses, arena games, the prairies and savannahs.

So long as injustice is meted on others; those they consider outsiders; those who do not look like them, they exercise a judicial closing of the official eye. Ephialtes has provided that assurance because injustice begets injustice, and likewise, trauma begets trauma. Gration sustains their commoditization of fellow human beings, ensuring new schemes are always in the pipeline. The tools and events they develop for mental wellness do not surpass the nyxian haze they emit and exhale every day.

Heracles, son of Zeus, (*pointing at the audience*) these people do not care for your Olympian idealism for the cosmos. They are content with imperfection. They transfer their impulsive nature to their children; they have normalized broken families and societies for generations. They feed their impulses regularly through get-rich quick schemes. We only show them how to outsmart the systems.

You don't need to look hard; where poor customer service dwells, Thoon & Agrius's coin washers abound and Eurytus has a growing client list. In these places, supply and demand as the drivers of business is a fallacy and the customer is never King; we, the Giants, are.

When it comes to money, Hippolytus provides them discreetly layered and untraceable offshore investments in tax havens and Pallas ensures it only reaches select cronies. Such is life.

[ALCYONEUS returns to center-stage, triumphant.]

Zeus should have warned you that my homeland Pallenes grants me immortality. String your bows tighter because all you Olympians have done is exhibit all the pulsating virility of a bunch of eunuchs in a harem of a second-class potentate.

HERACLES: (*Clutching bow, taking a shooting stance*) You forgot one thing, Alcyoneus. This is Samaismela, not Pallenes.

[DRUMROLLS erupt, followed by WAR TRUMPETS and THUNDER. TARTARUS appears stage left, a dark haze like a paper kite, swallowing ALCYONEUS as he braces for combat. He vanishes with a defiant cry. A momentary SILENCE grips the stage, then the SOVEREIGNS burst into ULULATION, waving placards and smartphones. The CURTAINS CLOSE to triumphant Drumming, cymbals and whistling of "Tate Taa taa"]

[A SPOTLIGHT illuminates the NARRATOR, who strides to center-stage in front of the closed curtains, exultant yet sobering.]

NARRATOR: (*To audience, with fervor*) The Gigantomachy ends—not with swords, but with sovereignty's song! (*CLAPS "Tate Taa taa"x2*)

Heracles, Samaismela's Sovereigns, fells Alcyoneus, last of Gaia's brood, with Artemis, Dionysus, Athena, and the Moirai weaving fate's thread. Tartarus claims all—Thoon & Agrius, Eurytus, Pallas, Gration, Alcyoneus—yet Alcyoneus' words linger.

(*Pauses, serious*) Greed, jealousy, impulsiveness—these are the Giants' true legacy, rumbling beneath Samaismela's lilies. The whistleblower, perhaps every citizen's voice, tipped this war. (Points to audience) But the prophecy's mortal? That's you—each who dares wield civic duty. Rise, Sovereigns, and cage these Giants forever! Who's your hero today? Name them!

[The NARRATOR exits stage right, humming the whistle's tune "Tate Taa taa". The stage darkens, DRUMS fading to a hopeful hum.]

***

ACT 6

THE CALL TO PROTECT

Setting: Celestial Olympia's gardens, a resplendent haven of ethereal beauty, bathed in golden light. Gazebos with white cornices gleam, draped in vines and shimmering mist. Marble paths wind through lush greenery, and a crystal fountain sparkles center-stage.

The 12 OLYMPIANS—ZEUS, HERA, POSEIDON, ATHENA, APOLLO, ARTEMIS, HEPHAESTUS, HERMES, DIONYSUS, ARES, DEMETER, APHRODITE—along with HADES, stand in their majestic robes, their divine aura radiant. The air hums with triumphant CHORAL CHANTS and soft LYRE MUSIC, celebrating the Gigantomachy's end. A faint WHISTLE echoes distantly, carrying the rhythm of "Tate-Taa-Taa!".

Characters in Act 6:
Zeus: Justice's pinnacle.
Heracles: The Sovereigns, global citizens.
Olympians: Hera, Poseidon, Athena, Apollo, Artemis, Hephaestus, Hermes, Dionysus, Ares, Demeter, Aphrodite, Hades.
Offstage: Whistleblower (implied), Sovereigns, Gaia (implied threat).

ACT 6 — |69|

[Lights up. The OLYMPIANS are scattered across the garden, chatting joyfully, their laughter ringing like bells. POSEIDON recounts a sea tale to ARES, ATHENA debates with APOLLO, and DIONYSUS sips from his goblet, teasing ARTEMIS. HADES, unusually present, stands near DEMETER, his dark robes contrasting the vibrant scene. ZEUS enters from stage right, followed by HERACLES, whose lion-headed headgear is now striking—its lion head golden, mane pure white, symbolizing his purified heroism. The OLYMPIANS erupt in APPLAUSE, converging toward ZEUS and HERACLES as they move to the back center of the stage. DRUMS pulse softly "Taa-Taa", building anticipation.]

[The applause fades. ZEUS raises his hand, lightning crackling faintly, commanding attention. HERACLES stands beside him, bow slung across his back, radiating mortal resolve.]

ZEUS: (*Voice resonant*) Olympians, gather around!

[The OLYMPIANS move to the back center, forming a semicircle around ZEUS and HERACLES. The CHORAL CHANTS soften, and the LYRE hums gently.]

ZEUS: Every ten years, a cosmic event shakes our realm. Rest assured, another looms—one to test us all...
HERMES: *(Grinning, interrupting)* I saw Dionysus shaking some vines already! (*Chuckles, dusting winged sandals*)
DIONYSUS: (*Raising goblet, smirking*) Yes, Hermes—the best harvest yet!

[The OLYMPIANS laugh heartily, HADES cracking a rare smile. The mood lightens briefly, then ZEUS' expression turns grave, silencing the laughter.]

ZEUS: (*Sternly*) But a matter demands our urgency before we resume celebrations. Someone hunts the whistleblower—the unseen force whose courage tipped the Gigantomachy's scales. Without them, Samaismela would still kneel to Gaia's Giants.

[The OLYMPIANS murmur, nodding solemnly. ATHENA grips her aegis, POSEIDON tightens his trident, and HERACLES clenches his bow.]

ZEUS: (*Rallying*) We must march to Samaismela—now—and secure the whistleblower's safety. Their voice, the Sovereigns' voice, is our cosmos' heartbeat!

ALL OLYMPIANS: (*In unison*) Hear! Hear!

ZEUS: (*Triumphant*) Olympians! Onward to Samaismela!

[The OLYMPIANS form a unified line, HERACLES at their side, and march toward the front of the stage, their steps synchronized to crescendoing DRUM ROLLS and CLASHING CYMBALS. A rhythmic WHISTLE grows louder, blending with the SOVEREIGNS' distant chant, "Haki Yetu! Haki Yetu!" (Our Justice!). The DRUMS and CYMBALS adapt to the chant's rhythm, pulsing with defiance. The OLYMPIANS' robes shimmer, HERACLES' golden lion head gleams, and the air crackles with purpose.]

[The CURTAINS CLOSE slowly, the WHISTLE's "Tate–Taa–Taa!" chant echoing. The LIGHTS FADE to black, leaving the audience in a charged silence.]

-PLAY ENDS-

ABOUT THE AUTHOR:

L. S. Njeremani is a social consciousness theorist. He describes himself as a human being in pursuit of heightened consciousness. A lateral thinker who observes that social problems can be solved best at the human level, moderate resolution at the generalist level and the least application of solutions takes place at the specialist level. As a multi-skilled individual, he deploys his talents towards thought-processes, debates and insights that inspire a second look at what has been normalized in conventional society.

Other Titles by The Author:

1. The Trouble with Kenya : McKenzian Blueprint (Vol 1 & 2)
2. McKenzian Blueprint (coloring book)
3. The Trouble with Kenya : McKenzian Blueprint (The Comic)
4. Ramani Ya McKenzie (kitabu cha rangi)
5. Utata Nchini Kenya: Ramani Ya McKenzie

www.ingramcontent.com/pod-product-compliance
Lightning Source LLC
Chambersburg PA
CBHW070439010526
44118CB00014B/2111